South American Scenes

Garrett Rittenberg

Bowery Books

New York

Copyright © 2019 Garrett Rittenberg

Bowery Books, New York

South American Scenes

ISBN For this edition: 978-1-7344202-0-3

Book formatting by: **Last Mile Publishing**

First Edition Published: December, 2019

For Linda and Gerald Rittenberg

Contents

Preface

It was my intention to travel around South America for a few months for more than one reason – a copious amount of curiosity, to spend some time away from Manhattan, to write about what I saw, and to fulfill my restless nature. Shifting from one place to another each day was something I had come to enjoy, and for whatever it is worth, with each journey I somehow felt I was becoming better at it. None of the previous journeys had lasted as long as I hoped, and my desire to take an extended journey only increased. This was to be at least four months of wandering across a distant continent, mostly overland, and entirely by myself.

I had come to find that once the desire to see a place infiltrates a person it is something that should be done while still fresh in the heart, for on some level, traveling and the desire to do so is a creative endeavor, and moments of creation are indeed precious. To think up an idea such as traveling alone across a distant continent takes heart, but to act on it takes nerve, and to try and make a book out of it takes a kind of grandiose passion. All of it together encapsulates a desire to make a journey last beyond its completion. Most of all, it is to live, but even more so.

I had been inspired by several writers who set out on similar adventures, but it was primarily an idea I had whilst traveling through other distant landscapes. I possessed no grand designs of exploration, I was in no need of healing therefore this was nothing like an escape as so many journeys are that we read about today. I was merely looking for a place to wander and create some poetry from it through the people and places I encountered. In fact, my habit of wandering made me initially want to title this book, 'A Place to Wander' – but I felt it would take away from the life and culture of the places I had visited. After returning home I found that I would be doing the people on the continent a disservice by giving it such a name. It would have been an ungrateful thing to do, and therefore it only seemed right to find another name.

I knew that by the time I returned home and the more time passed since the end of the journey, my memories of it would weaken. The journey would cease to be a continuous experience and would inevitably fracture into scenes. I had done my best each day to combat this fracturing by keeping up with my diary, but a day here and there was missed when I was too tired from a long day of marching through some fields or arriving in a city after a sleepless night on a bus. Therefore, my journey to South America belongs to the past, but these scenes remain.

Garrett Rittenberg
February 5th, 2018, Pondicherry

1

São Pãolo

Not much changes from day to day outside the Catedral Metropolitana, especially the haggard homeless who lay about on the large steps giving off a vibe that wavers between threatening and nearly dead. Many of the homeless people that sleep in and around the Praça de Sé do indeed look as if they are dead. Face down, arms extended outwards, at times laying awkwardly across steps or their head hanging off a curb, a missing shoe, open wounds and visible sores. Some with clothes so dirty it looks as though they have been dug up and left on the street. The hauntingly aged faces of young drug addicts provoke more thoughts of death or something close to it. It is difficult to stand still, let alone sit down outside the cathedral without becoming a target of panhandling from one of these disheveled characters. Each request or impulsive demand for money to passersby is accompanied by either a dribble or a burst of saliva, depending on their level of inebriation. Some are so incoherent that it seems as if all they wish to do or are capable of is scaring the hell out of you. It doesn't take long to realize that it makes sense to keep moving, even if slowly, and not to make eye contact.

A few unpredictable and drugged up people can make any place feel more crowded than it really is. They are also much more noticeable than most of the people in the square who are busy getting somewhere. Wherever it may be, it is unlikely that they are headed towards the cathedral as there were only a couple dozen faithful speckled amongst the endless pews when I walked through the three large doorways at the front. The doors are kept completely open throughout the day and appear inviting, but the destitute and bedraggled don't dare go up past the last step and on to the large landing.

The amount of worshippers attending the mass felt pathetic even if it was late in the afternoon. Like any good non-worshipping visitor of cathedrals, I took a seat near the bulk of the faithful and pretended as best I could to blend in. The service itself was not all that inspiring and the old priest officiating stayed on course with the routine of mass, never straying into a vociferating political or moral rant like many other Latin American priests I would come to encounter. I observed the devout and hopeful faces pressing their hands together for some time, but my mind began to stray and I paid more attention to the interior architecture of the cathedral. The curved ceilings and domes were soothing and made me rotate my neck in an odd fashion as I surveyed from one side to the other. There was more stone than gold visible, often a rare occurrence in any large cathedral, and it seemed appropriate in a city so entirely covered in concrete.

The quiet of the cathedral quickly faded as the sounds of hovering and passing helicopters thundered through the open windows. Just outside one of the large windows where a priest was calmly sitting with an eager confessor, a loud and stifling shriek repeatedly invaded the air, but did not disrupt the service. Each time it stopped I hoped for everyone's sake that it would not start again, but it continued throughout the service. The worshippers and priests were unfazed by the thunder of helicopters and random shrieks. Interruptive noise was something that they were used to. The noise inside was more piercing and annoying than the barrage of sounds out on the Praça. I had gone into the cathedral to escape the city for a few restful moments but noises in quiet places, like a dripping faucet or music coming through a wall, are often the loudest kind. When I went outside expecting to see a construction site, I was surprised to find a man holding a bible, swaying slightly and screaming at the top of his lungs whenever he got the impulse. Each shriek seemed painful, not from physical suffering, but rather the mental sort.

There was a regular police presence that calmly patrolled the Praça in packs, no less than three to a group, men and women. They wore helmets and protective vests whilst dangling from their hips were wooden batons covered in dents and scrapes that had pieces chipped off, making it evident they had gotten much use. Even though the cops carried a combination of shotguns, semi-automatic rifles and large revolvers, the casual swaying of batons was much more menacing and authoritative. Anyone of their firearms could kill someone instantly, and all would be settled, but coming into contact with their batons meant dealing with a kind of interminable pain. The sound of helicopters that I had heard inside the Cathedral was much louder now and almost constant. When visible they could be seen inching downwards at times making it feel like a raid was imminent, though, nobody was fazed by the noise or the possibility of it getting too close to a building causing an accident. When I trailed behind some of the groups of cops on patrol it did not take long to find them getting into arguments, removing the homeless from shops and roughing up more than a few. To watch them up close, their aggressiveness was often nasty and heavy-handed, but when I stood atop a low wall and observed them from a distance I started to realize how futile these small groups of police were if the endless crowds of people were to unite or decide en masse to take action of some sort.

Far down the Praça underneath the shade of some palm trees there were plenty of people not rushing someplace. Crowds gathered around a variety of shows being put on by peculiar and slick individuals. Bible thumpers shout and do their best to sway their listeners with serious faces and an array of theatrical gestures. Others perform mediocre magic and card tricks or attempt to juggle various objects such as knives, bowling pins, books, or flame covered sticks. Each performer has about the same amount of spectators except for one man that is getting ready to jump through a circular plastic hoop with knives pointed towards the center leaving him just barely enough room to get through. He was surrounded by a large circle that was four people deep and inched closer towards the center as the show slowly progressed. The short shirtless man was muscular and wearing only a pair of shorts covered by a sort of pseudo-traditional Amazonian skirt made out of frayed tree string. The hoop with knives was about four feet off the ground and far too high to get up and through head first unscathed. He would have to make an extraordinary leap upwards then horizontally glide through and somehow complete a full-frontal flip from four feet off the ground or execute a perfect somersault landing on the hard cobblestone surface of the Praça.

The show was clearly one of anticipation, and the audience didn't seem too bothered by it. They already knew that this stunt was not likely to be carried out smoothly, but still wanted to witness a man in all his hopes and confidence just before failing, publicly. The man sucked in the crowd by carefully lining up ten yards from the circle only to claim he was distracted by someone in the audience and a few more minutes of trash talking got the crowd more interested. He carefully set his feet again as if there were an imaginary starter's mark then suddenly responded to a heckler with a dramatic rant and challenged the man to do it himself, but quickly reneged, saying he could never let the man try such a dangerous stunt. Time after time he lined up to run through the circle only to delay the act keeping the crowd's interest as they continued to inch closer. The hecklers, and a few others walked away as they began to see through his act, but curious passersby continued to join as their anticipation had only begun. Nearly half an hour went by when the crowd had inched so close that it had to be pushed back and the man saw that the crowd could walk away at any moment. The spectacle was losing its glare. He put on an overconfident front by shouting and flexing his muscles to make everyone know he was really about to do it. The stunt was for real and so was he. His body was tensed, and the stunt was suddenly over. Even though he got through the circle it was not pretty and he looked foolish. When he leapt through his torso was scraped by the dull knives leaving visible marks, but no blood was drawn.

A sudden look of disappointment was visible on the faces of all who stood in anticipation from the beginning. Half the crowd quickly dispersed into the current of the Praça, looking regretful of the minutes they stood around watching the foolish man. With an embarrassed expression and the demeanor of a wet cat, the man quickly tried to start the show again for the sea of newcomers looking to be entertained. The man's partner walked around hurriedly trying to collect money from people with a desperate expression on his face.

A few yards away a much smaller crowd peppered around a portly mustachioed and middle-aged man holding an open bible. There were a few others in the vicinity doing the same. He gave moral lectures and the faces in the audience were painted with serious and contemplative expressions. He would speak calmly for some time, but would eventually become more animated as the sermon drew on for an hour. In my limited Portuguese I could easily make out that he was condemning the lifestyles and sinful behavior of those around him and expressed the need to become more pious. "O Diabo," the devil, was mentioned often in a threatening tone accompanied by finger pointing at those watching and then downwards. I had seen this show before in many other countries, and this time was no different than the rest in that I was expecting something different to happen. I spent more time watching the man with the book than the man attempting to jump through a hoop full of knives. Over an hour passed before I had had enough and decided to join the tide of people flowing underground and onto the subway. Even though the man with the bible had a smaller congregation I felt that there was something he did better than the man putting on the stunt. Perhaps the mistake the knife man made was to jump through the hoop. The man with the book didn't let anyone see the end of his show. There was no end.

****

Things may not have been changing on the Praça de Sé, but Brazil was going through a disruption, caused by the arrival of the World Cup and the not so distant arrival of the summer Olympic Games. These events have gradually brought Brazil into focus on the world stage as a subject for salacious news, and often the media is guilty of highlighting the country's most eye-opening stories.

From these stories it is easy to come to the conclusion that Brazil is somewhat famous for its crime, not only because of how much of it there is, but for the unusual and often surreal manner in which it occurs. All sorts of weird stories of barbarity had sprung up in Brazil during the previous year. Perhaps this is not unusual for the largest and most populous country in Latin America that is often seen as a quiet place of delightful hedonism and mysterious exoticism, but the lights and cameras of a world event can spark the emotions of many and the spotlight can unintentionally reveal its more savage side.

In the northeastern city of Recife, a man was killed instantly when he was hit by a toilet that was thrown from the top of a soccer stadium onto the street.

Another savage incident occurred at a football match in the

northern city of Maranhão when a player angrily protested a call by punching the referee. The twenty-year-old referee then took out a knife and stabbed the player who would eventually die from his wounds at the hospital. When the news quickly reached the spectators, friends and family of the player rushed the field and tied up the young referee, then proceeded to beat and stone him, quarter his body and decapitate him. When the frenzy had ceased the young referee's head was left on a spike in the middle of the field.

Another incident was revealed when a video was posted online that was taken by a man wearing a helmet-cam whilst riding on his motorcycle. He ended up being pulled over by a pair of robbers on another motorcycle, the one on the back wielding a large handgun. At an intersection, shortly after the robber got on the bike, a nearby undercover police officer got out of his car and immediately shot the robber, killing him before he even got onto the motorcycle, his buddy on the other motorcycle quickly fled.

Along with freak incidents of savage crime, there had been a wave of protests erupting in the big cities over the past year leading up to the World Cup, often with violent results. In fact, it was not just World Cup protests that were the scene of violence and chaos, but even protests carried out by groups such as teachers unions and other various labor unions that were turned into scenes of rioting, looting and destruction as a result of the marches being hijacked by anarchists and criminal groups using the presence of large crowds as an opportunity to rob nearby banks and shops. There is a group said to be called the Black Blocs that is responsible for turning many protests into riots and scenes of looting, but no one knows who they really are, who the leader is or what they stand for. This sort of mythical description of agent provocateurs seemed to fit into the story line of Brazilian crime. Whatever their true identity may be, they were certainly opportunists taking advantage of the rising emotions that came with the international spotlight. I wondered whether these stories were common or just random headline grabbing events used to stir people up as the start of the tournament came closer.

All sorts of security measures were being taken to prepare for the potential crime that could arise around the events of the World Cup, in response to the scenes of sudden of anarchy. Among them were an increasing amount of government conducted drug raids targeted at the powerful cartels in the slums and favelas of the large cities. There were even talks of putting up a wall near the Copacabana in Rio to protect beach goers from stray bullets coming out of nearby favelas. An increased police presence would also patrol the famed beach to lessen the potential for snatch and grab thefts or even to try to suppress mass robberies. Talk of crime about Brazil was as common if not more common than crime itself. But talk of crime has a way of spinning out of control much more quickly and in Brazil it appeared that it was the crime that was imitating the talk.

****

A couple nights before I was to leave Brazil, I lay in bed and was again greeted by the sound of thundering helicopters. After a week in São Páolo I was still not used to that noise that could only mean there was strife nearby. As the noise grew I opened the window of my room on the fourteenth floor and saw far down on the Rua da Consolação that a large seemingly endless protest had taken over the busy boulevard and the cars that were usually a constant presence had disappeared. Not much later I found myself walking in the boisterous yet calm protest. Every few hundred yards there were a group of drummers that gave a convivial mood to the young mass of people. They were on the street in opposition to the fast approaching World Cup. Walking alongside much of the protesting crowd was a nearly constant presence of riot police wearing protective gear and wielding batons. Their presence was dwarfed by the protestors and they looked an unavailing force for order. I wondered if this protest would end like the many others I had heard about and watched on television over the past year. The crowd was animated and cleverly expressed themselves, but I was weary and could not help but think it was all a front before they would create chaos, or it was created because of them. Collectively they carried banners that spread across the width of the street and as high as fifteen feet. There was even a man in an oversized Brazilian soccer uniform with a giant skull for a head ten feet off the ground.

As the crowd carried on down the large boulevard, anti-government and anti-World Cup slogans had been spray painted on the sides of buildings. Billions had been spent by the government in order to make the world's largest soccer tournament a reality, and there was a growing opposition to the staging of such an event when many felt that the billions could have been allocated more meaningfully. It doesn't take long to walk around São Pãolo and see that more money should and could be spent on improving the lot of people in the sprawling slums that surround the city.

Some protestors had specific demands along the lines of spending for education or health care, others more colorful such as, 'Fuck FIFA,' carried more simplistic expressions. The two-word slogan was one of the more common pieces of graffiti freshly painted on the buildings that the protestors passed by. FIFA was the protestor's real target, but even though targeting an organization such as FIFA seemed rather hopeless, it did not dishearten the crowd of young kids. A number of other frustrations and demands were being expressed by many. Signs for gay rights, and both sides of the Israeli-Palestinian conflict, as well as calls for action on global warming and messages demanding fairer treatment for the tribes of the Amazon. It was a mass of people perhaps united by their collective derision of FIFA, but fractured in its desires to express, at times opposing views on a number of other issues that are frequently shouted about in protests that regularly take place around the world.

After walking for about a mile amongst the crowd the sound of an explosion could be heard a few hundred yards ahead. I was suspicious, yet the crowd was not fazed. Brazilians seem fazed by nothing, I thought. But then more explosions occurred a few minutes apart, each with more force and the distance much less. These were stun grenades, but if close enough the sound was very intimidating and effectively split the crowd into a smaller, less threatening force. Still moving forward, I noticed a number of people starting to walk the other way, and in the long lights beaming down from hovering helicopters was a rising cloud of smoke. The police had begun to throw tear gas. When the smoke came closer many in the crowd no longer walked the other way but began to run accompanied by the sound of more stun grenades. I ran, too, and found myself running alongside well prepared cameramen wearing gas masks who continued filming amid the melee. When I found myself back where I had originally joined the crowd there was a large pack of ambulances tending to those already suffering from the effects of the tear gas at the back of the protest. The stench and sting of the tear gas grew steadily and there was not a cop in sight. Eventually the mass of the protestors had been turned around and marched back down the other side of Rua da Consolação. They were now louder and more determined, but eventually dispersed when they converged onto the equally large Avenida Paulista. The city swallowed up the young protestors, because in São Pãolo, it is easy for a hundred thousand people to disappear into the night.

Rua da Consolação was left empty of protestors, while the sting of tear gas lingered above the flickering lights of idle ambulances was all that remained. The cars returned and the street looked as if it had forgotten the crowds, and their demands and chants were an even more distant memory. It was a sudden wave of expression and emotion, something I couldn't help but think was suggestive of Brazil itself or even of much of Latin America. The potential for anarchy and chaos was ever-present, and the injuries received by protestors and police meant little to the city. São Pãolo would go on being itself.

****

I was not to be in São Pãolo for long. My journey across South America would not start until I left the hardness of the Brazilian mega-city. From São Pãolo I would head south stopping along the way to Ushuaia then head north seeing as many places as possible. I knew of a few places I wanted to see and would make sure of it that I did, but I had no real plan or frame of time in which to do it.

São Pãolo is an infinite stretch of concrete that has as much life as the most dense and greenest of jungles, and I did not mind getting lost and gradually finding my way around for a few days. Its endless high rises, graffiti, abandoned buildings, new constructions, and people of all stripes were more than enough to help me acclimate to the continent. Having lived in a couple and visited many, I often felt that cities never lie to you. Not that nature necessarily lies about anything, but cities are often given a bad reputation. To many they are the culmination of all that is evil or wrong with human society and are often considered the creators of illusions but it is not much of a stretch to realize that it is people who force their illusions, and delusions upon cities and everything else. For all their co-existing beauty and repulsiveness, they are brutally honest about people and cultures. To a lot of people cities are ugly, but the absence of nature often means the presence of what has been created by people, and the sounds of any city that many cannot stand are melodic to me. Nearly everything I would be seeing along the way would be new. And with that often comes a kind of upheaval in oneself. Some places would be thrilling, while others would be disappointing.

I was usually not reluctant to go anywhere, but like many that set off on a journey for several months or even years I had a lingering hesitation. It was a familiar place I had wanted to revisit, because I was not quite ready to leave New York. All the dangers of traveling were ever present in my mind; as well as being foreign, knowing only one language, not knowing anyone, being isolated, and a large amount of time with all of them was what I had in front of me. I was looking forward to a few of those characteristics of travel but not knowing when the either pleasant or burdensome aspect of each would appear induced anxiety and doubt. São Pãolo was a long way from New York but it was still agreeably familiar enough that I could feel as though I was slowly wading myself into the rest of the continent.

I went to São Pãolo because I had been there two years earlier and it reminded me of home. I was also curious to see if all the buildup to the World Cup tournament would have made any great changes to the city. But two years is not a long time in the life of a city, and it seemed that the more that went on in São Pãolo the more it stayed the same. There was nothing interesting to me about the fast approaching World Cup tournament. I had no interest in being surrounded by the crowds of face painted hooligans from every country or the chanting and horn blowing drunks that make up the bulk of spectators at any soccer match the world over. I was sure that over the next month I would find myself sitting quietly in some bar or cafe only to be suddenly surrounded by a hoard of jerseys chanting and shouting at a nearby television. I did not take it seriously. Perhaps in some way I was more like the kids on the Rua da Consolação. Except I had no cause I was fighting for, I just wanted a place to wander for a while.

2

Uruguay

The long oceanfront road paralleled by a walkway that stretches around Montevideo from one side of the city to the other is where many residents of the quiet city go when they are not tucked into their apartments or small houses. Restaurants are nearly empty, the bakeries are out of everything but coffee and pre-packaged cookies, and on a Friday night everyone is in bed by eight o'clock; Montevideo is such a sleepy place that at times it looks abandoned. I tired myself out walking across the city for three days, but on the fourth day I found myself well rested and again wandering along the Rambla which was littered with joggers running past one another just as well-bred dogs were being walked by freshly groomed people, and in front of luxury apartments overlooking the ocean a burly bunch of young men on a well-kept Rugby field were getting ready to play American Football.

Giving it a double take, I soon realized it was not just a pick-up game but a league match in full pads, helmets and jerseys with referees in Zebra-striped shirts. Players were lined up in military columns doing various stretches and warm up drills and with the field set beside the ocean it looked like it could have been California or Florida. Hearing the coaches who were the same sort of screaming drill sergeant types that so many football coaches tend to be, brought back anxious memories of my teenage years when I was on the receiving end of such disciplinary barking. It was strange to see that they are no different in Uruguay and even more bizarre to hear players being shouted at in Spanish, and not some brutish American accent. No matter how familiar the game was to me, American Football being played outside the United States was an odd sight. It is how perplexed Europeans tend to generally view the game no matter where it is played, because of the large amount of padding and the helmets that make players appear to be dressed like gladiators or astronauts. The scene could easily have been the set of a commercial for the National Football League. One team was indeed very good and executed their plays with discipline while the other ran around like they were blindfolded as is common among people who are new to wearing the awkward padding and helmets.

I was nearly certain that this was a sight I would only see in a neighborhood like Pocitos. There was not a chance of this taking place in Ciudad Vieja or even the poorer surrounding neighborhoods. There was a sense that only the well-off do things that are foreign and are generally out of reach for the poor. Locals are the poor and unless they are immigrants, they live with devotion to the things they have done their whole lives and are a part of where they live. Exploring other cultures is a luxury. I was well aware that I was enjoying that luxury and was uniquely exploring another culture exploring my own culture.

After watching the first half of the football game I decided to go for lunch at the bar of a nearby seaside restaurant, but as I continued along the Rambla I noticed each telephone pole and light post was covered with election posters. Trucks and vans cloaked with stickers and placards that showed smiling candidates with not too catchy campaign slogans underneath. Oversized box shaped speakers were tied to the roofs and beds of pickup trucks bellowing out electioneering rhetoric polluting both the beach and city. Young campaign workers in matching t-shirts handed out flyers on each side of the Rambla and went car to car at intersections making sure not to miss anyone before the light changed.

Any sign of an election is good if not relieving, especially in South America. After all it was not long since much of the continent had been governed by scowling mustachioed Generals wielding revolvers who were often removed and replaced by another General of a comparable description in a far too similar fashion. But there was no sign of tin pot dictatorship in Uruguay today or in the rest of the region, the age of the banana republic is gone. The Generals on the continent don't want to rule countries anymore, they don't want the responsibility of having to run a country. The only regime left in Latin America run by men in military uniform is headquartered in Havana and with the sitting presidents of Brazil and Argentina both being female, the region looked quite different than it once did not long ago.

****

Before I could even order a drink at the bar, I was having a political conversation with an old man named Pablo. He walked alone along the Rambla most days by himself and was pleased to have someone paying attention to him. In a restaurant overlooking the ocean, large families sat down at long tables having tranquil conversations. At the bar, he sat next to me and appeared far too dressed up for the warm sunny weather. His expression gave an air of being half-drunk for thirty years and looked as though he had wanted to be in London wearing an overcoat to cover his blazer, buttoned-up sweater, shirt, and under-shirt, each a different bright color and the light brown shoes nearly matching the jacket. Few paid attention to the soccer match on the television and the election flyers I had been given by all the different campaign workers were sticking out of my notebook that rested on the bar.

"Who is going to win?" he joked while tapping on the flyers with his tattered middle digit. Without removing his finger, he looked up for an okay to borrow them. I was indifferent and he began casually reading through the short paragraphs that summed up each presidential platform. Before I could respond he began talking about each of the candidates in a way that revealed his politics more than the candidates themselves did on their flyers.

We discussed each candidate in the election, none of which he was satisfied with and he was more bored than anything by them. Knowing next to nothing about all of them I tended to agree. The only politician he wanted to talk about was the one he hated. A snarl came across his face when I mentioned 'El Pepe,' the nickname of the current President, Jose Mujica. He did not see it as cute or funny, after all it is difficult to see enemies in such a way.

"We came close to getting rid of him more than once," he said with a regretful expression. But the attempts he spoke of were not recent. Pablo had been a part of the ruling government's police department that was in power in the 70's and was often a target of Mujica and his fellow Tupamaros movement, a group sponsored by Fidel Castro. The conflict in Uruguay in the 1970's was much the same as every ideological struggle that took place on the continent during the Cold War. There was a right, and a left, and their tactics, violent assassinations, torture, were none too different from the other. Whomever was in power treated the other violently, and whomever was out of power was violently seeking to once again grasp it. The only difference in Uruguay to other Latin American conflicts was a matter of scale. Uruguay was and still is not a territory widely sought after by any great power and today still holds little clout in the battle of ideas. But nonetheless every battle of the Cold War was given some degree of importance.

Political conversations led down murky paths, I always thought, but Pablo was not a talking head on television, he said he had done more than talk about politics. And he played a game that went beyond casting a ballot or making a campaign speech; he was a foot soldier, a torturer, an enforcer, possibly a murderer. For men like him life often came to an end in a similar fashion to the way they ended their enemies. But he had survived, and I succinctly realized that after talking to him. It proved successful in making him appear more like an accomplished man rather than a street scouring brute.

His tactics were politics at its most extreme, tactics that can only be described as a means to an end, which was indicative of what politics has always been for much of history. One group violently removing another. For most of the continent's history this was its political process, South America has known little democracy.

I was usually bored by political conversations, but for every political stance he spoke of it was often followed by a story involving him and his henchmen, doing battle with the Tupamaros and Castro and of course Mujica. His exaggerations were obvious, but the stories were good if not entirely convincing.

When I pressed him on his own group's violent methods, he became frustrated, and said quietly, "these people are smart and calculating."

"What political movement isn't?" I challenged.

"These men are smart," he said again implying that it was a not just a matter of them being well read or obtaining a bachelor's degree, but in a deceitful and deceptive manner. He was quiet for a few moments as he drank his rum then said, "they used to rob banks. They would kidnap diplomats and civilians." This was all true, but the very enemy of Mujica and the Tupamaros movement was guilty of the same offenses and often brutally so. It was a war therefore no side was without atrocity and ruthlessness. There was little room for moralizing.

"There are some, you'd be surprised how stupid people who want power can be. Remember many people lose at politics."

Pablo had not run out of stories, but rather had run out of energy. We were both drunk by mid-afternoon, he more than me, and his stories were becoming more exaggerated. Before I could make an excuse to get back to my room for a long nap, Pablo was saying 'Hasta luego' to all the waitresses and the bartender. And then finally to me. He stumbled out onto the Rambla.

And then I did, too.

It was an odd experience to speak with a stranger about the terrible things they had done, but they were the things he had done, and everyone likes to talk about themselves at some point.

When I woke up late in the evening, slightly hungover, I found some newspapers to read in the lobby of the small hotel. Ciudad Vieja was quiet and everything was closed except for one nearly empty cafe. I sat in one of the booths reading articles about Mujica.

I knew little about the man, other than a few articles and Pablo's derisive take on the President nicknamed El Pepe. A fat man with a face like a cat, and a slight resemblance to Raul Castro.

Mujica's age and stout grandfatherly shape made him appear harmless, but he did have a past unlike most elected leaders. Violent people don't always appear violent or menacing, but that was Mujica's past, and he certainly associated with people who were more brutal than himself. His image as a man of the people was not merely maintained through his political positions but also his paltry salary, the old VW Beetle he drives and his living on a farm on the outskirts of Montevideo instead of the official residence reserved for the President in the capital. He worked beyond the clock to convey a certain image and came to be labeled by the media as the world's "humblest," and "poorest" President.

There are few election posters with his name or face on it even though many newspapers and television shows were littered with stories about him. No one was using his name to get elected, not even his own party, which was peculiar because the front page of every newspaper was covering the President's visit to Washington. A rare occurrence for all this media attention and a standalone meeting with the President of the United States for any Uruguayan leader. Though, not overtly discussed with the media, the meeting supposedly had much to do with an ongoing lawsuit brought against Uruguay by the Philip Morris Co., because of laws that have supposedly taken a swipe at the pockets of the tobacco giant in an effort to get Uruguayans to smoke less. The suit was rumored to be upwards of twenty-five billion dollars, but members of the government put the number closer to five billion. Either way, were Uruguay to lose the case, it is a crippling amount for a country of only three million people.

The give and take nature of all things political was in the air during the meeting, as it was announced that Uruguay had agreed to take six prisoners formerly held at the Guantanamo Bay. Though, this and the Philip Morris case were largely overshadowed by the quirkiness of Mujica himself. He looked out of place in his suit and opened shirt, tieless, and even more out of place in the Oval Office. He was a man more suited to the end of a bar telling stories than dressed in a suit and being escorted into the White House.

The papers carried quotes by Mujica that day, the kind of lines that almost any man of seventy-eight might make when given a microphone, or in his case, several. Mujica's grandfatherly character and his statements were equally quirky and blunt, similar to the unconventional way Castro likes to respond to interviewers. Among them, "give a hug to all the farmers of California for me." While telling Americans to smoke less he also said to, "learn Spanish...because the strength of Latin women is admirable and they will fill this country with people who speak Spanish and Portuguese, too." He also went on to say that Latinos needed to learn English, too. But with regards to the legalization of Marijuana he was statesmanlike, "what we are trying to do is create policies that allow us to take the marijuana market from the drug traffickers, but that doesn't mean we are going to allow this addiction to spread."

These were small political solutions and like much news coming out of Uruguay it was quickly forgotten by the American press.

****

As eager and rambunctious as the volunteers that dotted the sidewalks and traffic lights to campaign, politics in Pocitos came across as a futile hobby, for everyone had all they needed, and the election was merely a popularity or beauty contest. The past political firestorms that Mujica and Pablo had spent decades waging were long gone and there was little reason to lift a finger in anger on this part of the Rambla. Everything was agreeable. The opposite was true at the other end of the Rambla.

There were no elections signs or volunteers jockeying for votes in the streets of the older, much poorer end of the city known as Ciudad Vieja. This neighborhood was filled with old buildings whose designs were of a similarly eclectic style to those of Havana and shared the same run-down crumbling face to its Cuban counterpart. Some kids in well-worn clothes played soccer against the walls of the depressing buildings of Ciudad Vieja, while others run around with mischievous faces, seemingly up to no good. Each kick of the ball sent a bellowing noise into the nearby boarding houses where junkies and the homeless stumbled to and from. Dogs polluted the air with incessant barking. The constant noise was maddening, but is gotten used to by those that live with it or know no different. The ocean is close by and can be seen down the length of some streets but everything about this faded neighborhood faced inward. At bus stops, there were long lines of people with sad and tired faces. The views provided no comfort or escape from the lack of any kind of the prosperity that exists a couple miles down the Rambla in Pocitos. Some buildings have exteriors like the insides of fire places, others decay more gracefully as they do in Havana carrying a tragic beauty, but gazing at them or the framed views of the sea is risky with the sketchy characters that appear around corners and idle in doorways, while drunks on stoops hold their faces in their hands leaving few places to seek refuge. Everyone I spoke to both in Ciudad Vieja and elsewhere warned me to be gone from this old section of the city before nightfall. It is a neighborhood where only the locals are allowed to idle. But I stayed as long as I could and watched a youth soccer match.

The rambunctious crowds of parents and friends watching ten-year-old boys play soccer as if it were a professional match was a drastically different sight from the few who lifted their heads from a newspaper to gaze at the American football match in Pocitos. Soccer was king in the middle class and poor neighborhoods and every dramatic turn led to wild shouts from the crowd and a goal led to a nearly five-minute stoppage for celebrations. The parents were passionate, one running onto the field, causing a coach to get red carded, forcing him to watch from under a tree a hundred yards away. A crying goalie gave up two easy goals bringing disappointment to his father and fellow onlookers, while the other team had huge celebrations, piling on top of each other. These were the poor of Montevideo and did not have the luxury of other cultures, just that of their own. These were Uruguayans.

****

The next day I was in Colonia del Sacramento, often shortened to

Colonia in conversation, a pretty little town that had been fought over by empires and settlers for centuries. A few modern streets lined with stores filled with all the necessities that run into the little cobble stoned section near the water is all that remains of the old city with trees growing on faded colonial buildings of the old town. There were cobblestoned streets and restored colonial buildings covered in ivy and dramatic trees with purple leaves growing onto them. Stray dogs could be seen fighting or having sex on every block and old abandoned cars were used as large plant pots and makeshift greenhouses. Little ladies with small tea shops served cakes to guests out of a room of their homes turned into a cafe.

I walked around the entire old town in fifteen minutes which led to going around numerous times and bumping into others doing the same thing, wishing there was more of it left to see and wander amongst. It would have been nice to get lost in the charming little town, but it was easy to become familiar with the entire place in an hour. Everyone finds their way to the water where there was once a grand port but now a long narrow dock with hobby boats slowly wobbling alongside each other like toys in a bathtub. Including one from Wilmington, Delaware.

Old men brought chairs to sit and fish on the rocks furthest from the shore almost completely surrounded by water that fused with the clouds speckled in the sky, causing the horizon to blur. No one bothers anyone and the atmosphere is decidedly tranquil. Everyone was basking in the solitude of this quiet sunny country. It is impossible to foresee a problem that could not be easily resolved.

The nearly constant view of the enormous river makes it appear as though it is the edge of an island. It was indicative of the whole of Uruguay being separated from the continent. A small isolated place, a giant green cloud hovering just above the water. It was an island whose purpose was merely to separate the Atlantic Ocean from the Rio de la

Plata. A place hidden from the world and even its own continent, where the people are soaked in solitude.

In Colonia, with its busy port of ferries coming and going every hour, it was inevitable to look west to Buenos Aires and the rest of the continent. Montevideo and Colonia were both like an appendage of Argentina and it is no coincidence that from its very beginning it was governed by the province of Buenos Aires. Uruguay has a peculiar presence on the map, and one wonders why it exists at all. It could easily be a part of Brazil or Argentina, but the reason it does exist is little different than that of most countries of the Western Hemisphere. It was another case of men wanting to govern themselves and not be controlled by an oppressive elite, near or far. Both were under Spanish rule, but the initially larger and more developed port of Buenos Aires naturally came to control the undeveloped area of Uruguay then known as Banda Oriental. The area around present day Buenos Aires however, quickly grew its own elite governing body and wealthy landowners, who came to see the settlers across the Rio de la Plata more as subjects than as fellow settlers. Its scarcity of people has always been a factor of the formation of its character from the beginning of its settlement. In fact, the Spanish did not even begin to settle in the territory until one hundred years after the Spanish explorer, Juan Díaz de Solis made landfall.

Whilst sitting in Colonia it was difficult to believe that the city was once the largest port city of Banda Oriental. After a couple of centuries of fighting between Spain and Portugal for control of the port city Colonia del Sacramento, Montevideo was created as a new port in order to keep shipping in business whilst the fighting raged. It is difficult to imagine a ruined city before it was ruined. The Spanish brought around one hundred settlers from the Canary Islands to start what would become the capital of Uruguay. Though, Colonia del Sacramento was still a key port and with the gradual rise of

Montevideo and a firmer grip on the city, the Spanish eventually decided to destroy Colonia so the Portuguese would have no reason to continue seeking control of the profitable port. The tactic was effective and Portuguese influence in Banda Oriental declined.

Growth came to the territory by way of pillaging, cooperation and cohabitation with the local Indian tribes. Its abundance of open land was ideal for cattle grazing which was more or less the sole reason for the gradual settlement of the territory, and since Banda Oriental neither possessed nor produced any desirable product, it was the main source of development and the small framework of an otherwise frontier economy.

After the settlers of Banda Oriental and the Indians came to mix with each other, it was more or less the beginning of an identity that would bind them to the land on which they grazed cattle and inhabited permanently. It was not long before there was a cattle boom and Banda Oriental's unused land became too enticing for would be cattle grazers not to take advantage of. Settlers mostly arrived from Buenos Aires Province, then gradually more so from Spain. Even though they were both Spanish colonies and ultimate power was in the hands of the Spanish King, the larger of the two colonies was given the freedom to govern over both territories as it saw fit. There was almost an immediate discord between the settlers of Banda Oriental and the visiting cattle grazers of Buenos Aires. While a number of the settlers from Buenos Aires Province stayed for good, there were a great deal of them that would return across the Rio de la Plata as they pleased, never acquiring any connection with the land and only saw Banda Oriental as a place of business or worse, a place to exploit, thus the permanent residents were seen in a similar fashion. As profits increased so did governance and control by the local bureaucrats of Buenos Aires Province. This inevitably led to rifts between the two Spanish Colonies. Rifts that not only resulted in violent clashes but would leave a lasting mark on the character of the people of Banda Oriental. The permanent settlers would come to be defined by, and united in their opposition to overbearing rule and governance by Buenos Aires Province. Alas, it was not only overbearing taxes and generally rough treatment that frustrated the settlers, but a growing condescension from the supposedly more 'sophisticated' Buenos Aires men of property that started to irk the settlers.

As much as they disdained the cattle grazers from Buenos Aires Province the sparse population of Banda Oriental was largely dependent upon them as a source for economic growth. The character of Banda Oriental was that of a frontier or a Wild West. The settlers and Indians alike had little to no desire to develop agriculture, which kept population growth as well as the economy and society stagnant for centuries.

In one of the few histories of Uruguay in English, the historian Francisco Bauza, talks about the culture and conditions of Banda Oriental's earliest years that led to a lack of development and barbarity amongst the settlers for a few centuries. Not only were the economy and societal growth stagnant but the settlers were deemed barbaric by the not too distant settlers of Buenos Aires as well.

In John Street's history of the independence of Uruguay, *Artigas and the Emancipation of Uruguay*, he gives blunt descriptions of the lives and society of Banda Oriental in its earlier days. Street has several amusing descriptions of the settlers that some historians may have been too afraid or likely too shy to mention. The men, he describes as living lives of perpetual campaigning between the Spanish, Portuguese, and Indians who fought one another or formed alliances against in order to weaken the other, creating the perfect atmosphere for revolutions. Of the women, he says they, "were scarce and of the few that were around," Street describes them as being "barefoot and sluttish like the men."

He goes on to say that, "like all primitive, scattered peoples...hospitable to any chance visitor...but so isolated they become distrustful and cunning...Their pastimes were their vices...drinking, gambling, robbery was commonplace. The wild shoot-'em-up territory where self-preservation and impulsive behavior were the dominant culture that lasted for centuries." Street contented the imperial powers were a modernizing force, unintentionally.

As for matters of faith, Uruguay has always felt a distinctly different impact from religion than its neighbors. That is, very little. Uruguay is not a haven for priests as are the poorer and more populous countries of the continent. From its beginnings and throughout its history, Street amusingly explains that Uruguay was a place where religion was, "rarely practiced...if they (gauchos[cowboys]) went to church they sat outside on their horse listening." It was amusing to read this, because on a Sunday morning in Montevideo, I came across a rather drab Church that looked as though not much money had been put into its construction. There was no traffic going in or out of the Church, nor did it look like there was even a service schedule. But across the narrow street there was a steadily growing crowd of supporters for MWFC, Montevideo Wanderers Football Club. The Wanderers' headquarters was a beautiful Beaux-Artes building, with a large satellite dish on top. The people of all ages wore large black and white flags as capes, while waving another flag or blowing into a plastic horn. Cars and buses could barely get through the small street and at times paused to celebrate with the Wanderers fans. They all posed for a picture for a photographer across the street and continued singing. It was mostly young men casually dodging the cars and buses squeezing through the crowd. Passing bus drivers honked and waved. A heavily pregnant woman with huge swollen breasts danced to the beat of the drums. Soccer was more of a religion than the church could ever be.

Uruguay is not an evangelical nation nor one deeply entrenched in the workings and beliefs of the church, and as civilized and orderly as its towns and cities are it is still a kind of Wild West, a small independent country, built on one being able to bask in their own solitude and freedom, beholden to no spiritual institution. Even with a small population compared to neighboring countries, Uruguay is still largely empty and uninhabited, the character of its people is decidedly pleasant if not docile. With the exception of a few poor neighborhoods, there was hardly a menacing place in the country, there is no more savagery. The political warring is done with, the fighting with Argentina long gone, and it is no longer pulled back and forth between Spain and Portugal. The internal political clashes that existed during the Cold War are gone and forgotten by the young and only remembered by its aging veterans. Political battles are happily if not fiercely fought at the ballot box. There is little reason for strife in Uruguay, because why fight when one could stroll on the Rambla.

My last night in Colonia was one of perfect sleep, which made me even more ready to see the continent. I sat in the modern ferry port that had the atmosphere of an airport, eagerly awaiting to depart for Buenos Aires. I was convinced there was no more restful place than Colonia del Sacramento and had I been coming from the other direction it would be a perfect getaway from Buenos Aires. A perfect place for an affair or some sort of secret life. No one is nosey and everyone keeps to themselves. It protects you from the normal hassles of a crowded city or a crowded life. I later realized that Montevideo and indeed all of Uruguay was a relief from the noise and congestion of Buenos Aires, from its craziness, from its traffic and congestion. Yet I was feeling the pull of Buenos Aires, and as pleasant as Colonia was it was impossible to look across the Rio de la Plata and not be drawn to Buenos Aires and the rest of the continent. Across the river was a city and a continent, large, loud and entirely unknown to me.

3

Buenos Aires

As the boat bounced across the Rio de la Plata, my journey across the continent had officially begun. Even after stopping through São Pãolo and Uruguay this was certainly more of an entrance to the continent than arriving by plane. São Pãolo was familiar to me, and Uruguay was so disconnected from everything, it may as well have been a hovering green cloud, and far too pleasant to be considered entrenched in the continent. I knew I would only reach the continent by crossing this river. The water's muddy disposition brought forth thoughts of an unquestionably foreign place. A river the color of mud was disconcerting, the life beneath the surface an even more unsettling mystery.

It was only a few days after my arrival in Buenos Aires that a plane had crashed into the river a few miles north, killing some automobile executives. Helicopter video of a small private jet crested on the top of a small island in the river was tragic and worrying, and would somehow confirm my suspicions of the river being a magnet for death.

Before the boat docked, my ears were infected with the cluttered noise of traffic and the sight of skyscrapers. Part of me wanted to return to the tranquility of Uruguay, but I felt uneasy and nonplussed about taking the same boat journey. I had survived the rough crossing and it would be foolish to turn back.

My curiosity pulled me across the traffic plagued highways and into the grid of streets. The city was a familiar and agreeable sight that required little adjustment. Besides, standing at the beginning of a journey filled me with both physical and mental energy enough to wander for days.

It quickly proved an easy place to settle into without having to try very hard. Any city was somehow always familiar to me. Every block had a welcoming cafe or restaurant and the streets were bustling and happy. I found my way to the Retiro neighborhood and settled in for a week. I laughed at how easy it was to enjoy life there and how any apprehension of being a foreigner was more than distant. The city was undeniably loud in many places and having just come from the near silence of Uruguay I was happy to find that I quickly adapted and was capable of enjoying the different decibel levels of each side of the Rio de la Plata.

I had searched for a description of the city and found that more than a few people liked to mention how Buenos Aires was South America's Paris or more specifically the Paris of South America. The Paris of South America, just how Beirut was the Paris of the Middle East, I thought. Every new world city has its degree of old-world infusions, but yet still remains something all itself. As soon as I read it I was suspicious of the comparison and my doubts only grew the more it was repeated. It was a comparison I was unwilling to accept. On the surface, to the superficially inclined and to the indifferent this is supposed to be a sort of compliment or badge of honor, but it is more cliché than anything, and in a way renders a dissatisfaction from the start with what Buenos Aires might really be. Surely any city that seeks to be like any other is not much of a city.

The phrase is said in a manner that more than suggests one would rather be in Paris. Which is unfortunately true of Buenos Aires, but this is not done with other cities. Where does New York remind us of? Or San Francisco or Rio or Mexico City? A great city is better off being something all to itself and incomparable to any other city. This comparison has gone on for well over a century, starting around the time when its governors started to seek to make it more or less a replica of the city on the Seine, most obviously through architectural means. It also assumes that Paris is what all cities strive to be. It is a tough argument to contend with for there are worst cities to be compared to, but one reason above all would be that any city that tries to be like any other city is ultimately lacking.

I could not resist the dueling question of; Does the comparison work the other way? This beggars another mischievous question; Is Paris the Buenos Aires of Europe? Does Paris seek a more Argentine character? I think that kind of retort exposes the snobbery of the initial description. The comparison does little good for the identity of the city and says more to what it is not, which is to say, it is not Paris, but rather something that has a slight resemblance of a place we would all rather be.

Once I had decided to no longer think about Paris, I walked into a large antique market where I was reminded of the large antique market at Port de Clignancourt, one of my very first memories of Paris. All old junk looks to be related to each other, and the junk in Buenos Aires resembled the junk in Paris.

I was carrying nothing with me and the sight of all the stuff that once belonged to people long dead came with a sense of relief knowing it was not mine to deal with. I would not have to suffer the boring fate of looking at it day after day. I realized that even in this big city that I walked around for days, I was idling too much and sure that wandering a more difficult and open road would prove more fruitful. I was pleased that I did not enjoy such pastimes. Wandering through it and the rest of the city was more enjoyable. I did not want to live amongst stuff. I bought a book and continued wandering.

Buenos Aires was busy, but it was an easy place to relax and my discovery of an amiable little cigar shop only pushed me further towards watching the city go by. It was situated off a loud street only a few blocks from where I stayed in Retiro and mostly sold every kind of Cuban cigar which appear more enticing and exotic to American eyes. Instead of buying a few cigars I bought one or two at a time as an excuse to go back and talk to Esmeralda, who owned the shop. She loved to tell me how they ship Cuban cigars to America with different labels to avoid the bureaucracy and restrictions. "Anything you want, anything, we can ship to New York or Switzerland. It is no problem. Sometimes we ship through Canada."

She had cigars to sell, so I could not blame her for making a pitch each day, but much of our conversations were political by her own inclination. She was the kind of person who looked for every opportunity to complain about the politicians she despised most. She hated Obama and the current Argentine President Christina Kirchner. At times, there was not much in the way of conversation for she often spoke in paragraphs. Kirchner never seemed to have any great supporters among the people I had spoken to in my first few days in the city. Her recently deceased husband Nestor preceded her as president and even to the most indifferent outsider the transition of power from husband to wife, even through an electoral process looked a shady proposition. The Kirchners' political power is not based in the capital for they hail from Rio Gallegos in the south, a stronghold of workers unions in the industries across the southern provinces from whom they derive much of their support.

Esmeralda spoke in the same fiery way that Kirchner did, and they shared a decidedly similar style. They would both start with delightfully soft tones and expressions before quickly reaching something that could only be described as pugnacious. When they argued, they did it as a kind of goading challenge. The eyes widened and the chin slightly raised, an argument was akin to a knife fight or a encounter with a bull. They were bold and ardently expressed themselves.

Esmeralda ranted of the corruption of the Kirchners and the incompetence of Obama. After a few days I was more entertained than intrigued by her political fury for she rarely offered up much of an argument. Though, each day I heard her talk of such things, there seemed something more tangible to her ranting and vitriol towards the Kirchners. Buenos Aires looked a prosperous place in most every way. Surely it was not a place of desperation or extreme violence like some other cities on the continent. Even after spending a week in the city it was hard to recognize the economic turmoil Argentina was currently in. The country was run on a debt ridden and thus imploding economy headed towards national default and bankruptcy. To make matters worse, many of their creditors were American and European hedge funds. The Kirchners were often accused of corruption and estimates of their personal wealth always hovered around $100 million. The more I listened to Esmeralda and the more I read about negotiations between the government and their hedge fund creditors I felt more certain there was something rotten in the state of Argentina no less so than in the House of Kirchner.

I had little with which to challenge Esmeralda on her one-sided rants. She resembled that ever more common character in the United States of someone who only watches one news channel and more or less parrots what they hear from it. I decided to take her arguments at more than face value, for they were far more than I could contribute to a conversation on Argentine politics.

One night, I was restless from all the tobacco and needed to somehow get it out of my system. I went for a late-night walk, heading in the direction of Plaza de Mayo. Much of the streets were suspiciously empty, and the people I did see were all hurrying in the same direction. When I was a few blocks from the Plaza de Mayo there were crowds of people that grew larger and louder, and I quickly found it was all in celebration of Argentina's Independence Day. I had only seen the plaza completely empty during the daytime but now it was impassably full of people under a star filled sky. All of the surrounding buildings were now lit up with colorful lights. I slowly moved through the boisterous crowd, and realized it was not just a celebration that came with beer and the strong smells of oversized meat smoking on coal fired grills, but with political groups rallying in the square trying hard to make their statement heard and presence felt.

The Tupac Amaru Barrio Group was more sinister and less jovial than any other and much of their statement was derived from their intimidating demeanor. They held up black and white checkered flags and wore matching vests with a picture of their Peruvian Revolutionary namesake, that is Tupac Amaru II - recognizable from his more modern tall hat, not his Incan predecessor. Unlike many other groups or other people celebrating in the square the members of the Tupac Amaru Barrio Group had stone cold faces, and stared down whomever they looked at. They called themselves a social organization group, but they were more like a localized mafia that controlled the poor districts of Buenos Aires.

There was a stage set up at the east end of the plaza where a few musical acts performed one after the other all celebrating and riling up the crowd for Independence Day. A dramatic tango show was put on for the cameras. I managed to get close to the stage and I was only separated by the Tupac Amaru Barrio Group who made their presence felt at the front. President Kirchner came on stage to give a speech and rile up the crowd even further. I had been listening to Esmeralda rant about this woman for a few days and to now catch a glimpse of her somewhat humanized her but ultimately, she still looked very much the shifty politician. Perhaps in another setting she would espouse a motherly quality, agreeable, but the only thing unquestionable was her posturing and posing speech. It had all the trimmings of a disingenuous politician. Only sycophants could have been moved by such a person.

Afterwards, there was a massive fireworks display that nearly covered every square inch of sky over the plaza. The fireworks were louder and more forceful for they were also the lowest fireworks I had ever seen, only about a couple hundred feet higher than the surrounding buildings.

Though much of the crowd cheered at her presence they all carried banners for opposing candidates, they were patriotic but had other plans for a future leader. Even though Kirchner would not seek reelection, her party's candidate would go on to lose to Mauricio Macri of the Republican Proposal Party. It would only be a few more months before the Kirchner era would come to its end.

4

Buenos Aires and Borges

It was easy to enjoy Buenos Aires but my only goal if I had one at all while there was to get a sense of Jorge Luis Borges. Buenos Aires proved an easy place in which to do nothing and get little done, perhaps another comparison to Paris to consider. There were plenty of people hurrying some place or working very hard, but it was a place of leisure. A place to shop and browse, to spend all your money in a few hours if you wished. The abundance of people sitting in coffee shops encouraged me to do the same and going from one cafe to another made for happily full days. I quickly became no different than everyone else - why not sit, eat, drink, talk, and watch everything float by. It was all too easy to find company, someone to talk to, a girl to flirt with, and at times someone to politely argue with. It is possible to spend weeks on end walking around the city to new neighborhoods, some interesting, others menacing. With this kind of atmosphere there was no better thing to do than get lost in the world of Borges.

I had prepared for my travels by bringing a book I would always find interesting no matter how many times I read it. If I was stuck in transit and sought to escape for a few hours I could always take it out of my bag to entertain myself for an hour or so. If any cafe ran cold or a bar emptied out I always had something to do. I was more than okay with the fact that my sole accomplishment in a week in Buenos Aires was reading the collected fictions of Jorge Luis Borges. The moment I put this book in my bag, I knew I would never feel alone or at a loss of what to do.

I had prepared little in way of reading about the city itself, but before leaving home, I had read a great deal of Borges and nearly everything I knew of Buenos Aires was through his stories and other various writings. This could be an irresponsible way of learning about a place, but there's no one else connected in such a way to Buenos Aires as is Borges. He belongs to this city in the same way Joyce belongs to Dublin, only more so, and there is not much else a city could ask for than to be the setting of the creations of such a man. For him Buenos Aires is the background for stories about time and human nature that in a way make it a city for all times and all people.

I initially thought the only reason to go to Buenos Aires in the first place was to see where Borges had lived, to get a taste of the air he had breathed most frequently, and take a look at the last building he lived in to get a sense of where many of his stories were written. Besides, I had no desire to see a gimmicky tango show.

Borges made every writer, thinker, artist, governor or man of action seem dull and pitiful. This is made all the more interesting by the fact that he was blind for the second half of his life, and spent much of his life before his blindness as a librarian. Borges' stories were more interesting than nearly everything, including the whole of Buenos Aires. I traveled with a small library that consisted of a few books, but mostly it consisted of Borges. By regularly reading this book, I was reminded that one book of his collected fictions is a library in and of itself.

While walking through the Retiro neighborhood of his later years I could imagine the old man, blind and well-dressed being slowly escorted around by his wife or a friend while the people honked their horns and hurried in all directions, telling them mind blowing literary anecdotes that leave one contemplating everything they had ever thought before, because nearly every Borges story leaves one with the feeling that they have just had an epiphany.

Each day, I spent a few hours wandering the city, but the more I read and reread Borges' collected fictions the more solitary and drawn into the pages of the book I became and the less I wanted to see of Buenos Aires. These stories cause the mind to spin and look at everything in a decidedly different fashion. I was failing as a traveler, but I wanted to be in the world of his stories; that of knife fights, mirrors and a never-ending library. When I finished the last page of his complete fictions I had lived a hundred times and traveled thousands of miles through the past, present and future. None of the stories are more than thirty pages, and sometimes less than a page, but are endlessly fulfilling and equally stimulating. I had even attempted to memorize a few of his shorter stories.

After finishing the last story, I started the book over again, jumping through to my favorites and then rereading the others. I did not just do this while I was in Buenos Aires or even just in Argentina, but until I finished my journey. On a few occasions I read short Borges stories twice in twenty minutes, and the rest of the day was spent thinking about them and I was completely satisfied in doing so. Borges stays with you in a way that most writers never could, it is like seeing a beautiful girl you can't get out of your mind or hearing a philosophical phrase espoused randomly from a mad-wino that puts you off balance, turns your eyes sideways, but you are now more clearly focused, forever. He is a writer you cannot forget or unread even if you forget the details or the plot of a story. The feelings they incite never subside.

When I went looking for the Buenos Aires of Borges I quickly realized it was long gone. Much of the culture and society that had influenced him took place in a city that was much smaller and a part of the machismo obsessed era of the 1920's when scores were settled in alleys and often came to fatal conclusions.

Not too far from Borges' Retiro apartment in an upscale neighborhood, the city's most visited site is the large Recoleta Cemetery. Naturally I went there, looking for something of Borges. I ventured out to the cemetery sitting in its most upscale neighborhood and surrounded by a large cement wall on all sides, it was a cemetery that more resembled a miniature village filled with marbleized mansions.

A cemetery is a marvelous and thoughtful place to wander and La Recoleta is so large it is its own microcosm within the city. With the extravagant tombs placed so close to one another it resembles an open-air museum for the dead. It is set up in a grid, robbing it of any sort of wonder or mystery, just like the city, I thought.

No matter where they may be, an extravagant cemetery is a kind of theme park for the dead, an odd exhibition of what some people do with a great deal of money left over. The tombs at Recoleta were sad monuments to people who could afford a monument to themselves. As aesthetically pleasing and peaceful as the cemetery was there was something utterly absurd to it. Those that had oversized tombs built for themselves and their families, must have thought to do such a thing in order to be remembered or give some sort of extra importance to their otherwise forgotten lives, but the grandness had the opposite effect and made it quite easy to forget all about the people at rest inside.

I looked for Borges in the strange way anyone looks for the grave of someone they never knew. After reading all of Borges' work I felt I knew the man at least more so than the hundreds of others buried in Recoleta. I was aware he had died in Switzerland almost thirty years before, but mistakenly thought he had been buried in Argentina's grandest place for its dead. One of the gardeners disappointingly confirmed my mistake, by saying, "Esto en Suiza," which made it seem a few planets away.

It is a peculiar feeling to be in the city of a man such as Borges and not find a single thing in his honor. Since he died in Switzerland and is buried in Geneva there is no grave to walk by to contemplate. There is no statue to the great man as there are to countless prime ministers and generals, albeit some of them mad men like Rosas, who did his part to execute thousands of Argentines in his ruthless twenty-five-year reign. It goes to show what countries hold dear. There was not even a plaque.

Though, I never found anything honoring his work or memory, I found his name being used rather than celebrated, but some would argue the reverse. There is a large upscale shopping center with his name emblazoned on all the windows. Whether his name is used by the public or is tacked onto the side of a building, it does not make his stories, his voice, any less exhilarating. It only succeeded in making the owners of the mall all the more desperate and uninventive. It was hopelessly commercial. It was like a mall being named after Albert Einstein. Even Picasso would have been a more acceptable name for such an endeavor. It is hard to believe Borges would not have wittily insulted the naming of a shopping center after him. Perhaps in a similar way to how he described the Falkland Islands War between Britain and Argentina as a conflict between, "two bald men fighting over a comb." It was odd more than anything. Perhaps a library or a university would more naturally suit the man famous for among other fictions, a story about a never-ending library. But this looked more than an opportunistic business ploy to bring name recognition to a shopping mall. Borges is indeed, as V.S. Naipaul says, Argentina's best man, and on the whole admired by his fellow Argentines. It does not make his stories, his voice, any less exhilarating, nor cheapen his brand or his name. No matter what is done with his name, his stories transcend any attempt to purposefully or unknowingly tarnish or misuse it.

My affinity for Borges was not merely for the works he created but for the bookish life he led. Having lived the solitary book loving life he did before he became blind and even more so afterwards, it meant that he spent a great deal of time within his own mind, in the worlds of the books he read and later that were read to him by faithful helpers and curious visitors. Borges' life and work is not just a lesson in itself, but it is a lesson in the importance of books and a good library, either public or private. By reading his works I also came to see more vividly that it is possible to create a world of one's own through reading and writing without seeing most of the earth, and a grand world at that. One does not necessarily need to see the highest mountains to have fully lived. All the young men need not march off into the trenches in search of glory; a life without action can count for something, too. Borges' stories and the life of the man himself, gave me pause, and made me contemplate even more what I was doing on the road, doing my best to get across a continent and back. I was in the midst of doing the opposite of Borges' life, my aim was to traverse a continent. But for a week I lived in the world of Borges' fictions in the city where he lived much of his life. By reading Borges, by re-reading him, and at the same time traveling a great distance to places I had never been before, I felt a glutton for experience and adventure. I was content but still my curiosity urged me to start moving south into Patagonia. I would soon leave Buenos Aires but Borges would undoubtedly remain with me.

Though, I could connect in a way with the long gone Argentine, I had failed to connect in any significant way with the Buenos Aires that sat before me. I did not find the heart of the city, perhaps because I was much too concerned with finding something of Borges or because there was not much there to be had. Either way I was satisfied in looking for something of Borges there, for I did find something of him. I had failed to find his grave for it was not there, but Buenos Aires, is and perhaps there is no better monument to pay eternal homage to him than the city itself.

With this, I felt satisfied with how I spent my days in Buenos Aires, no more so than after reading a few lines of Borges' poetry:

> 'this city which I believed was my past
> is my future, my present;
> the years I've lived in Europe are a delusion
> I have always been (and always will be) in
> Buenos Aires.'
> *Obra Poetica* (1964)

5

Xinjiang Bomb

The old men sitting in a large cafe in Retiro had nothing to do and I sat with them passing time while waiters in vests and bow tie navigated between tables with trays held next to their ribs. There was a sudden appearance of smokey images on the large television behind the bar with news of a bomb attack at a market in Urumqi, China. I quickly grew anxious wondering whether it was the same market I had had breakfast at every day for a week less than a year earlier. Not many pictures of the carnage were on the screen, but in the few that were released I could easily recognize the street where the market was set up each morning, only now, people were laying dead and blown up next to abandoned food carts and debris. Was the debris from abandoned vegetables that had been dropped in the melee or was it body parts? The news of the bombing was quickly gone from the screen and the images changed to some other distant conflict. I had been in Buenos Aires for a week and seeing many of the same people each day now made those faces in Urumqi much more vivid. I could not take my mind off the vibrant market and the city and that part of China, Xinjiang province. The market was still familiar and seeing the dead bodies was like watching footage of my own house burning down. The news inspired irrational fears and my hands instinctively touched my knees to check if the rest of my legs were still attached. Being lucky has always been an ambiguous phrase to me, but I momentarily understood it while looking at the images on the screen.

Walking out of the cafe, I thought nothing of Buenos Aires. The city was now grey and quiet and appeared to be abandoned. I looked at no one and went for a walk to think of what I had seen in Xinjiang. The idea of traveling across South America had come to me while crossing overland through the desert of western China. It was a strange idea to have even though deserts do tend to spur illusions. I put it down to a remote place encouraging one to be in other remote places, like mountains causing mountain climbers to seek other mountains. Either way, the market was still quite vivid to me.

Around two thousand people would gather early each morning on the narrow street to cook, eat, barter and socialize which made the market a small refuge from the congestion and pollution of the city of Urumqi. It was as though the countryside of Xinjiang province was briefly passing through the city and when it was gone the street became hollow the same way any street feels after a parade has gone through. Truckloads of garlic were unloaded into wheel barrels and onto men's backs, butchers took meat cleavers to whole carcasses of lamb hanging from iron rod stands, industrial size pots of noodles were cooked while half a dozen bakers stacked fresh disc shaped bread. The market was loud with the sound of everyone speaking in a congenial tone. It was a place where one could communicate without having a common language and thus I became friendly with a few of the food sellers. A trio of old bearded men looking like wizards sat together on a corner gawking at me like an exotic bird and I did the same to them. After the second day we shook hands and laughed at each other thinking of how unique it was for us to be crossing the same path, let alone a few days in a row. Much of the pleasure of the market was in watching the people and everyone was in fact being watched while eyeing someone else. All took pleasure in recognizing others and for me it was a pleasure enhanced by being a foreigner.

On the road to Urumqi I stopped in Turpan in order to see the ruins of an ancient Silk Road city called Gaochang and then the small traditionally Uyghur town of Tuyoq. Outside the main market in Turpan I found a taxi driver named Ablat who agreed to take me to both towns. Ablat was a Uyghur with an aggressive face, a big mean smile and a body that made it evident he was well fed. We were around the same age and he was astonished by how much I bargained for where I was asking him to take me. I had a small book of words in Uyghur and we gradually started to communicate, asking each other questions through the book and hand language as well as writing things down. Our silences said something, too. One of the first things I asked Ablat was why he did not have the small beard like most of the Uyghur men whom I had seen in Turpan. He drove in front of a small police station and explained that four Chinese policemen had held him down and shaved off his beard, which he further described by slowly sliding the side of his fist around his jaw from ear to ear. Just as we got outside the limits of Turpan there was a large development of nearly finished apartment buildings fit with solar panels on the roofs, but no one living in them. There were enough for 100,000 people and Ablat's face began to frown as he said they were all for Han Chinese migrants from other parts of China and not for Uyghurs like him. It did not take long to realize the many differences and grievances between Uyghurs and the Chinese, and it was quite clear that being a Uyghur was something that did not gain one privileges in Xinjiang province, much less any other part of China.

As we went further into the desert the only thing to see were emergency shelter shacks, but at one point on the other side of the highway were some military vehicles heading towards Turpan. What started off as a few trucks continued for three miles with every kind of military vehicle, including tanks which were being hauled on flatbeds as well as trucks full of soldiers. The government intended to keep its grip on the city not just through building housing for Han Chinese migrants.

The little town next to the ruins of Gaochang was a relief from the unforgiving desert that it was surrounded by. Patches of green trees brightened the dusty streets and like any poor village there were happy school children and the smell of meat cooking on makeshift grills. Alongside the road were the weathered faces of men and women laboring contentedly, like artists, slowly chiseling and shoveling the earth away as if they were carefully crafting a sculpture. Their muscles memorized the motions of the work, which allowed them to relax their necks and often look in another direction while working.

Two miles from the town was the colossal site of the ruined city. I had never even seen a picture of it before and only read a few accounts of what some had found many years earlier. What I found was none too different than what I had read. A lonely man in plain clothes selling tickets out of his pocket stood at the entrance like it was an abandoned theme-park on the moon. The money I gave him went into his pocket, which left an uneasy feeling of being had, but there was nowhere else for it to go.

The beige rock structures of the city bubbled up from the earth and were difficult to approach. It was a confusing place to walk around after driving through a desert. Where was one supposed to start? The city looked like a cave that had its ceiling cut off or had somehow risen up through the ground. It felt appropriate to want to ask Ablat if we were actually underground, but with the glare of the sun and a clear sky overhead it would have been a foolish thing to say aloud. I fully expected white bats to be flailing passed at any moment. The city was so large it was difficult to get a sense of its size from the ground that I had to just go further and keep moving. At times, it was necessary to climb some of the structures, about thirty feet up in order to see how far the city spanned, which was about three miles long and two miles wide.

Ablat and I continued to slowly communicate with one another as we walked around the ruined city. He pointed out some of the more significant structures and encouraged me to take pictures in front of them. Each time I asked where the Buddhist temple was he would abruptly make a scowling noise like a cat, clearly expressing his disdain for anything Buddhist. It was an impulsive sound of disgust like he had been taught or conditioned to react in such a way. The mere mention of Buddhism brought out his prejudice and dislike for any religion other than Islam. When we reached the circular Buddhist temple made of stone there was Arabic script carved into the exterior walls which gave the peculiar appearance of a kind of ancient graffiti. I pointed out the carvings to Ablat and a prideful grin slowly grew on his face knowing it had been both conquered and desecrated by Islamic invaders long ago. Again, he encouraged me to pose for a picture, not because of the temple itself, but because it was covered in Arabic graffiti and likely because all the Buddhists were gone.

A small group of Japanese tourists came through on a horse drawn buggy. They were the only people we had seen in two hours and he sneered at them as they passed and then gave them the finger when they were far enough away to see. Anything he did not like he would give the finger. Like any bigot, he hated more than one thing…Russia, China, Buddhism, and many of the other things we slowly discussed. Though, his hatreds were mostly local and at the furthest they were regional. When I mentioned places like America, Brazil or Israel, he was indifferent. The rest of the world was much too distant for him to hate.

The sun was glaring, and it brightened the light colored rocks making them even paler and thus putting a greater strain on our eyes, but I could also see Ablat's face much more clearly. He had the playful yet brutish disposition of a boy who was about to burn ants with a magnifying glass. A bully was built in the same meaty way, though he was not quite that, but just as eager for a playground scrap. Again, I thought of how well fed he looked, because no one else nearby looked anywhere near the same way, except for myself I suppose. When he saw a bird sitting on some distant ruins, he picked up a rock and tried to hit it. Every rock he threw made him look more like a child and thus completely innocent. Anyone throwing rocks looks childish, I thought. We started laughing and then I tried, too. There was little chance of hitting the bird and our wild attempts were making us laugh more with each rock that landed astray. We were too far from the bird that sat confidently and un-phased to have a chance at hitting it. Ablat gave the bird the finger.

I could feel him wanting to test out his bigotry on me when his questions turned more towards religion. He wanted to know my religious affiliation and he was slightly confused when I said I did not have one. The Chinese were atheists, but that's not how he saw them. Being Chinese was a religion in and of itself, especially to a Uyghur. A non-believer was not something he knew how to be mad at. Even though he didn't seem to care too much, I quickly changed the subject to his family. The sudden change in subject made starting the conversation bumpy which meant we spoke in numbers, at first. He had one wife, was married for six years, had two kids, and was thirty-three years old. Gradually we were back to a more interesting pace of conversation and his eyebrows became busy and he gave a mischievous laugh when I said I was not married.

After a few hours of wandering around the ruins we drove another ten miles into the desert towards Tuyoq. It grew hotter and drier and trails of dust lingered in the air from overpacked trucks that had long passed. I was happy to have seen the ruins and was imagining what we would find in Tuyoq. The road was unpromising and with the exception of an occasional signpost and some refuge shacks there was only distant mountains to keep one's attention. More sand now covered the narrow road as the car carried us through the desert and towards oblivion.

A small spec far down the road slowly became a large shack built as a military post. A mustachioed soldier with long hair wearing black fatigues stopped the car with a casual flick of the wrist. He looked like a mercenary. At nearly forty years old, his long hair and facial hair seemed like privileges one gets when serving after the required years of conscription. His face was burdened from years of reporting to superiors. A row of riot shields leaned against a small table where three young soldiers with shaved heads dressed in full protective gear sat bored with empty stares. The riot shields were perplexing and looked like props, but there tends to be a legitimate reason for having a riot shield on hand. In the middle of a desert road there was no riot let alone people to be seen for miles. It made the scarce desert seem full of potential hazards that one would not usually find and also gave the feeling of being watched through a scope.

One soldier idled, while another was playing a game on a laptop and the mustachioed soldier instructed me to hand my passport over to the more serious looking of the three. The young soldier carefully examined the pages, stamps and visas from places like Brazil and Uganda, slowly rubbing his thumb over the seals that had been pressed into them. It was obvious he could not speak English, nor could he read anything other than the Chinese visas. He carried a forced look of obligation and was stalling in order to convince me that he was honestly weighing the decision. It was a bad act and as the time dragged on both Ablat's face and mine carried looks of disappointment and frustration. We lingered there saying nothing and only the wind spoke. It felt absurd. The soldiers were very quiet and spoke in short and tired sentences. A decision was made only after I inquired, and they looked relieved to be done with the two of us.

What I already knew, Ablat was about tell me, which was that a couple months earlier, nearly fifteen hundred Uyghurs had been killed in the small town. Ablat wrote '1,500' on a piece of paper, pointed over to the soldiers and then simulated a machine gun with his hands. The circumstances were murky, and the story was certainly gone from the western press. It was no surprise we were not let through even though I had no credentials as a journalist or any official government affiliation. I was just a foreigner with a Uyghur.

By the time I stopped thinking of China the streets had become dark in Buenos Aires. I wanted to be elsewhere and early the next morning I left on a bus for Patagonia. The bus roared the entire day and into the night as the highways turned into small roads. It was still dark when I was woken up at a checkpoint on an empty road by soldiers standing outside in the cold with M-16s hanging down off their backs and one tightly gripped a leash attached to a German Shepard. The dog was let off the leash and ran through the bus for a few minutes. Two young men were told to get off the bus and taken into a small building beside the road. The rest of us were searched and questioned. The two young men never came back out. We were allowed through and left without them. As we passed through the checkpoint and the city of Puerto Madryn could be seen beside the ocean, I still wondered what I would have seen in a little town in the middle of a desert called Tuyoq.

6

Dinosaur

Sitting beside me on the bus was an Italian man in his thirties named Antonio on his way to Rio Gallegos. Not long before I got off the bus in Puerto Madryn, he told me, "they found a dinosaur a few hours west of here." Somewhat stunned that he was suddenly talking to me, let alone about dinosaurs, after not saying a word for the previous twenty hours, I had no clue if he meant the dinosaur was found recently or sometime in the past. The only communication we had had was his offering of some of his dried noodles after I dropped mine in a trash can from being shook by the bus hitting a pothole, nearly scalding my hand from the water coming out of the steel tap next to the bathroom. The air outside seeped into the bus, making everyone shiver. Every temperature seemed dangerous and his offer of food was much appreciated.

He nodded assertively and tried to further make his point by extending his arm out completely in the direction towards the empty landscape but was stopped by the cold window lightly coated in frost. I asked him where it was located more precisely, but all he could say was that it was on a farm a few hours from Puerto Madryn. He was a potbellied and ragged young man with unkempt facial hair. There was a faint smell of whiskey that permeated from him, which he had been pouring into Coke cans he cracked opened throughout the journey. His small soup thermos reeked of whiskey, but he did not appear drunk, just relaxed.

As we talked, he drank and ate rapidly. No matter how casually he spoke, it was a rushed conversation as it was only twenty minutes before arriving at Puerto Madryn. He took an avocado out of his backpack, and then a set of keys out of his pocket. There was no pocketknife attached, and he improvised with one of the simple brass keys and started to push it into the avocado dragging it slowly around the skin. The keys dropped into his lap and unfazed, he finished the job by breaking open the avocado with both hands. He offered me one of the mangled halves and I politely declined. We continued to talk as he ate the avocado like an oyster. The back of his hand wiped the green off his face and the skins sat in his lap. He was a brute, an Italian vagabond, a traveler. The luggage disorderedly laying in front of him was a small backpack full of clothing and a long skinny black case that could only be holding a gun.

"They are beautiful creatures," he said, as if he had actually seen one alive.

The long black case and his description of them made it seem like he was about to go hunting for some dinosaurs to mount on his fireplace. But he looked nothing like a hunter.

"One day Patagonia will have no more dinosaurs and all the bones will be dug up and taken to London or America. They will be gone soon," he said sadly, and became quiet for a few moments as if in mourning, and then began speaking of himself. "I travel. I teach, too. I never went to school, but I work. Doing construction, as a football coach, and teaching English and Italian." He then said playfully, "I am an Italian, so I am basically an Argentinian."

Before I could ask him about the gun, what he was doing in Rio Gallegos or anything else about the dinosaur, we had arrived at the station, and those getting off the bus were hustled out the side door to make way for new passengers rushing onto the bus to continue south. I quickly said, goodbye, and he casually said "Adios." After the long ride I was suddenly disoriented. It was like being given instructions before heading out on an expedition or a dinosaur hunt. An expedition I was not prepared for. I had no tools or a map or any idea of how to look for a dinosaur. I was an unprepared explorer in need of tools, a whole new set of clothes and protective gear and some kind of scientific degree. The cold air of Patagonia was exhilaratingly fresh and overwhelmingly clean, and instantly rejuvenated my body that had been cramped and stiff from sitting on the vibrating bus since the previous morning. Breathing in the air had the same feeling as drinking cold water when thirsty. There was something distinctly different about it. Buenos Aires now looked a dirty and unhealthy place to be, littered with loud invasive noises and fumes. It was a different kind of arrival than the one I had had in Buenos Aires. Getting off the boat I was greeted by a small highway, with roaring trucks and impatient car horns. Even though I was lagging from the bus ride, the air gave me a second wind.

The sudden burst of conversation with Antonio still startled me as I stood at the station collecting myself. We had only spoken with each other for ten or fifteen minutes. But I could not help but think of the few things he said to me. I thought of the long silence between us which now felt like a part of the brief conversation. Even though nothing was said, it was a kind of beginning to the conversation. The long silence was now just as startling as the talk of dinosaurs. I wondered if he had waited to tell me about the dinosaur and himself just before I was to get off the bus. I knew that travelers could be quiet and cagey hoping to reveal as little as possible and just enjoy moving from one place to another. Other times information pours out of them and they feel the need to share the information they have about their surroundings. The loneliness accompanying them often makes them impulsively say things about themselves. That was what Antonio was doing, he was telling me all about himself after not having spoken for almost a day. He did not have a question for me, I was just his listener. He knew I had no choice but to listen.

****

Someone had recently found a dinosaur and I wanted to see it. When I looked for news of its discovery, I saw the headline, 'BIGGEST DINOSAUR EVER.' How could I have missed this with all the reading I had done in Buenos Aires? There were estimations of its size while alive, which were up to seventy-seven tons, the weight of more than fourteen African elephants and it was being called a "Titanosaurus." It had been found on a farm near a place called La Flecha, which I could not find on a map. It was not a town, but rather an area a part of a private farm or estancia. One of the workers had stumbled on it while clearing brush, and not much excavating was needed to realize it was not a rock or the bones of some large animal dead for less than a thousand years.

I failed to find a ride out to La Flecha from Puerto Madryn. Everyone kept saying it was a private place, which made it seem like a secret place. I got a ride down to Trelew to inquire at the Paeleontogocial Museum. I figured it to be the best and last place I could find information on getting to the farm.

Trelew was a sleepy town with gridded streets covered by the greyest of skies. The center was busy for a town of its size and a microcosm of a larger city center. Not much went on other than the slow business of restaurants, cafes, and small clothing stores. Though Trelew had a dreary face, the air was still decidedly fresh and intoxicating. Each deep breath was the equivalent of a B-12 shot. It was wonderful to be outside in the fresh air, my bus-lag finally dissipating.

This is what Patagonia smells like, I thought, fresh, clean, and cool. Not a new car smell, but something that had never been dirtied. It does something to the body. The toes are more in sync with the fingers, and the blood flows so fluidly in the body that it can be clearly imagined you can almost see it. The air was different, like that of a different country or at sea. There was an unmistakable purity to the air that brought to mind flashes from youth that carry no meaning like power lines and dead animals. Days when fresh air made you remember the things around you, cleared your mind, and helped you retain what you saw. They became more vivid and could easily be remembered. This air, too, made you aware you were no longer in Buenos Aires or any kind of urban setting. There was no such thing as a city anymore from this point of view. Cities were either impossible collections of waste or deformed growths that bubbled out of the earth.

****

On the main street there was almost a constant noise coming from a protest that circled the city. They looked out of place in Trelew. The few police in sight hung around and did not show any sort of presence or authority. Where was the power here? Only decisions could be made in places like Buenos Aires, and not a provincial town like Trelew. What use was a protest? All ages of mostly men walked in step chanting prepared cadences against mining and extraction activities going on in the area. There were drummers and loud bangs from single shot fireworks like M80's. It looked potentially violent. A man on the bed of a pickup truck was constantly shouting into a megaphone, directing the crowd.

At the museum I was confronted by a small bespectacled woman uninterested in anything but selling me a ticket. She was a bureaucrat who loved rules and lived in a dinosaur museum. My questions did not interest her much either when I inquired about the Titanosaurus.

"Is it possible to go to the farm where they found the Titanosaurus?"

She replied with a curt, "no."

"Why? Has everything been dug out?

"Yes."

"Where is it, now?"

"Well it's here, aqui."

I was thrilled to have found it so easily. "Can I see it?"

"Yes, but you must buy a ticket first."

I was stunned at my luck. I thought I would have to somehow bribe my way into being taken to a private farm or sweet talk the owner.

Leading me passed the reception desk just off the lobby she pointed at a large wall-to-wall window that looked into a laboratory filled with oversized microscopes and machines not easily defined as to what they were for. Old computers sat blankly, and files were stacked high on counters in a sloppy manner, waiting to be dealt with. Towards the back of the room sat what looked like a large red log on a wooden table. It was unmistakably the largest bone of the newly found dinosaur. Its redness gave it an alien character with some kind of life still pulsing through its thick red center. Are dinosaur bones naturally red? Around it were other bones somewhat smaller, either laying down or stood up in shallow containers and supported by a small pile of sand. I asked to get a closer look, but she would not allow me to go into the laboratory. I stared as best I could from that annoying distance, not close enough to see what its surface really looked like. I tried again but she was uninterested in me getting a better look. After she left me to gaze at the newly found bones, a man with a bored expression while eating an apple entered the room, and leaned against a counter as if no one could see him. Because of the glass that separated us, I waited for someone else to walk in and start the dialogue of a sitcom. The small viewing room I stood in was dark and the laboratory was completely lit up. Surely this was not a one-sided window, there was no use for that, and I could clearly be seen. I contemplated the possibility of the laboratory for dinosaur bones doubling as a break room. I knocked on the window to get his attention and motioned if I could go inside for a better look. He looked up with his expressionless face intact, thought for a few seconds and then with his hand that held the half-eaten apple waved me towards the door to come in.

His name was Norberto and he was tall and scraggily and absolutely unmoved by the presence of the dinosaur bones in front of him. He was merely someone who wanted to go home and did not feel like working in a laboratory any longer. He was an archaeologist, which meant he hated museums and laboratories and preferred the rigors and adventure of field work. The dirt is where the amusing work of the archaeologist is done. He had little to say, but one of the few things he did say was "I like to dig, no microscope." He also said that archaeologists need luck more than anything to find bones and artifacts. They need farmers and workers stumbling over things. A profession so predicated on the luck of things being found in the ground, the only other comparable thing I could think of would be oil, but even then, it takes less luck to find oil than to find dinosaurs.

Getting a closer look made any conversation with Norberto useless, something he seemed to understand. Norberto also understood what I was quickly realizing and that was to stop asking questions and spend more time looking at the bones. It was better to take the opportunity to look at the giant pieces of dinosaur in front of us rather than to talk about them. There they were, in plain view, not in the distance or in an archaeological photograph surrounded by fences of string. The largest bone was the femur or thigh bone, and for the most part completely intact. There was also an arm bone standing straight up almost two feet. The redness of the bones became pinkish under the direct light. It could be described in many ways and compared to many things, but the bones sat on a table like a cadaver awaiting an autopsy. It also looked like a small tree turned to red stone. The ends of it were perfectly cut and it rested the same as a tree cut down in the forest would and left to rot with bugs crawling throughout the inside. It also looked like a body hardened then stripped of its skin. The top end of the femur was the shape of a large ball fit for an equally large pelvic bone. Its flaky surface could be easily picked away but was clearly dense and still very tough towards the center. It appeared as though the muscles hardened because the blood had dried up and its redness remained. All dinosaur bones are red I confidently thought to myself. The redness gave the illusion that they were still wrapped in muscle, freshly cut off a living dinosaur. It was obvious that it should not be touched, but I immediately broke that rule when Norberto momentarily looked the other way. Its surface had the same unexciting texture of mixed rock but this was made better because it was a dinosaur.

If these were the bones, what were the muscles like? And the skin? The muscles had either been eaten or withered away in the very spot the bones were found.

I said Titanosaurus to myself, enjoying the new name of an old creature. Trying to make it more real, knowing I could never see one alive. I wondered what had it really been called, but quickly realized dinosaurs had no other names than the ones we gave them when they were already long dead. They were always named long after they had lived. Maybe they were not meant to have names.

After inspecting the bones and hanging around the museum for a couple hours, I became tired from the long overnight bus ride. Norberto remained sitting in the laboratory like a bored security guard and he had seemed to want to be left alone with the bones. I needed to rest, but I was hungry too, so I dragged myself to the center of Trelew to find something to eat. The grey sky had turned black, but many of the dark clouds were still visible.

I ended up in a Parrilla, which is a place in Argentina centered around grilled meats, not far from the museum and could still hear the protestors chanting as I walked through the door. The large restaurant was nearly empty except for a few quiet couples. The one waiter wore a cheap black suit and a bow tie hung low off his neck. The menu he handed me had two options, the descriptions of which I could not understand but could make out that one was larger than the other. I pointed to the larger one of the two options on the menu and asked for a glass of wine but was given a whole bottle from the region of Mendoza.

The restaurant was quiet except for the hushed conversations of the couples until a portly mustachioed guitar player began to strum out strange melodies which were dramatically interrupted every three minutes by the beaming sound of a loud horn that otherwise hung off his shoulder. The food took a while and I was forced to take in the odd spectacle of a one-man guitar and horn band. This led to me finishing half the bottle of wine before the food arrived.

A few minutes later the man blasted the horn loudly and a large plate of various meats piled on with bones sticking out of them was placed in front of me. I began gnawing at them with little regard for how I looked or what each piece of meat was. I picked everything up with my hands. I was a vagabond, a traveler and was happy to just be eating. I was a little drunk by then and steadily became more drunk no matter how much I ate. I thought of Antonio and his ragged appearance and I thought I must look the same. I did not care for it did not matter, everyone there was focused on something or someone else. I could not figure out what some of the meats were, they had peculiar shapes and there were lots of bones. When I asked the waiter, I could not figure out the translation of what he called each of them. It was not long before I drank the whole bottle of wine and the cork of another was efficiently twisted off. I again asked the waiter what each piece of meat was and without hesitating he said there was, "Raptor thigh, Stegosaurus ribs, and rack of Pterodactyl, and of course the Titanosaurus. You are the first customer to try it."

"Excuse me," I said.

"It was the dinosaur plate you ordered, señor. Did I make a mistake?"

I agreed so as not to tread down this path any further. I then thanked him and went back to eating and drinking. When he next came back to pour more wine I asked what kind of wine it was and where it was from. He said, "it is the blood from the dinosaurs, of course. They only use grapes for wine up north - down here we use every piece of the dinosaur for our meals, including the blood for the wine."

I did not know whether to laugh or curse at the man. I simply said thank you wondering if they were just having fun with a foreigner.

When I walked outside it was dark, nearing ten o'clock and the anti-mining protest was still circling around Trelew. The relentless protestors were drumming, shouting and continued to set off disorienting M80 fireworks. The long swath of people blocked the one street I needed to cross. Only a foot or two separated the protestors front to back and some waved flags, held signs or played instruments. The parade of people looked endless and I decided to push my way through which did not please the few I bumped into. A few shouted at me, others tried to antagonize me by patting my shoulders, and one lady softly pushed me from behind.

★★★★★★★★★★★★

I had not been in Patagonia a full day and I felt like I was going through some kind of initiation ritual. All I wanted to do at that point was walk up the hill to my little room and sleep for twelve hours. But after seeing the dinosaur, eating what I was told was dinosaur meat and being pushed around by this crowd of locals I was going through some sort of rite of passage ceremony in order to be allowed into Patagonia.

I finally broke through the crowd and slowly walked up the hill, intoxicated by the meat and juices of the Titanosaurus. The small towns of Gaiman and Rawson, were both ten miles away in opposite directions, but in the empty streets, Trelew felt like a cold desert or a small town in Siberia, vulnerable to some lurking prey. Stray dogs would not leave me alone and tried to playfully gnaw at me and smell me. I knew they could smell what I had just had for dinner, because I could still smell and taste it. I scared them away by picking up rocks and threatening them, but throwing the rock was never necessary. They knew what it meant when someone picked up a rock. I made it to my bed, and I could barely sleep. All the meat writhed in my stomach and I was forced to listen to the protestors and their bombs.

****

I wanted nothing to do with dinosaurs the next day. I was hung over but eager to be outside and do something to get the alcohol and meat out of my system. Since there was little else to do in Trelew but visit the dinosaur museum, I decided to head west towards the Welsh settlement of Gaiman for the day. Rawson and Playa Rawson were also Welsh towns, too, and even Puerto Madryn had lingering touches of Welshness, but Gaiman, was supposedly the most Welsh of all these little towns that had been settled by migrants from Wales a hundred and fifty years earlier. The little town was a quirky presence in the wilderness of Patagonia, and it made me curious enough to walk the ten miles from Trelew. In its life of a century and a half it had still retained much of its Welsh heritage brought by the settlers. It was also made somewhat famous by Bruce Chatwin in his '*In Patagonia*,' where in a mere eight pages he vividly brought some of the townsfolk to life in not the most flattering of ways. The book was a success, but the people who had been captured by Chatwin's shrewd lens were none too pleased to be included in the public discourse of a man they had welcomed into their homes. Just like I searched for something of Borges in Buenos Aires, I looked for something of Chatwin in Patagonia.

I wandered through the little streets of Trelew and reached the spot where the city decisively ended with a row of trees corralling the city and its last poorly built houses. On the other side was an endless landscape partially plowed but mostly untouched. I questioned this small jaunt before setting off, even more so as I passed through the outskirts of Trelew and was repeatedly threatened by several mad-eyed German Shepherds held back by chains just long enough. I craved the solitude of a long walk, and the thoughts and peace it would inspire. There was little I sought to accomplish other than making it to Gaiman for it was pleasant enough knowing that no one else had this idea on that day. The freedom of walking in Patagonia and carrying nothing on my back was as liberating as anything could be. I wanted to cover some earth without the assistance of an engine or wheels and the mere thought of a solitary walk felt productive.

I could not see any sign of Gaiman for it was ten miles away, and I would come to find it had only small houses and was behind a hill. So I began to march my way alongside the road on the gravelly shoulder much too small for any kind of car to idle without partially remaining in the road. I was quickly consumed with the abundance of land that is Patagonia. The earth was hued in several patches of both bright and neutral colors. The sky was a bright light blue which made the whiteness of every streaking cloud much brighter and more pleasing.

The gravelly shoulder turned to grass and at times I was forced further from the road whenever a car or bus would thunder passed. By the time I swiftly walked three miles I knew this unbeaten path was going to be arduous even though it was flat the whole way. For one quickly comes to find that ten miles is a long way to march before noon.

I was none to bothered by the distance and I reveled in the little challenge I made for myself, considering each step a few feet further away from noisy urban life. A step both from cities and further into another world.

No matter how straight the road was on the map, during the whole of the ten mile journey, I could not help but think I would likely get lost from a kind of mental fatigue or that repetitiveness would cause me to choose another direction at random just to stimulate my mind.

Pickup trucks could be seen in the distance bobbing up and down on dirt roads away from the main road I walked. They left small dust trails that only lingered for a short while. The roads led to private estancias, which were usually cattle farms. Most of the dirt roads had 'no trespassing' signs and appeared to have no end for they usually stretched onto and over distant hills. They were a spooky presence for it would take trucks nearly ten to fifteen minutes to reach the distant hills, before finally disappearing over them.

The same bus driver passed me a couple times during the few hours I walked giving me a supportive smile like I was trying to swim to Florida from Cuba or the English Channel. He honked and gave me a motivating thumbs up. In his eyes and to the sleepy passengers, I could only have looked mad and irrational, for there was little reason to walk all that way and perhaps his smile was one of admiration that I looked like a person guilty of taking a rebellious route on a conventional path.

Not only was I getting closer to Gaiman but I was slowly sweating out the alcohol, meat and confusion of the previous night. I thought nothing of the day before and was fully consumed by the immense distance ahead of me and the simple details of all the nature around me.

After walking about six miles I found myself wondering why there were so many dead dogs along the road to Gaiman. There were several kinds, often the domesticated type and the agony or peace in which they had expired was paused in time, for they were somehow even more still and at the moment just before death amongst the stillness of the empty landscape surrounding them in every direction. A Black Labrador was torn into several pieces; its intestines strung out and dried out across the grass like black electrical tape. One was flattened perfectly at the edge of the road by a car or truck that gave it the appearance of a small rug, its facial expression was less than fraught and stuck in a moment before it got a chance to realize it was about to die. Another puppy that appeared to have died a few minutes before I saw it from natural causes in the most peaceful way was without any external damage and at first glance looked to be sleeping. I could not help but think that it had died from abandonment and had starved or dehydrated to death. There were others in various states of expiration, but it was both eerie and sad to think how they had gotten out to such a seemingly random place. A number of them had inarguably fallen prey to another animal. The domesticated kind could only have run astray or been abandoned and forgotten. I was sometimes walking in a graveyard and stopped to look, probably longer than I should have or would have if it was anywhere but this isolated spot. There was no one to tell you not to do so and even then, you were almost forced to look when they were in your path and you could see them in your sights for a couple hundred feet.

There was an inevitable strangeness to finding so many dead animals in a field. The specter of death became palpable and the surrounding countryside no longer possessed a simple beauty, but a complex and ruthless undercurrent of natural selection. Then I realized I was alone and vulnerable to this empty place and its elements, seen and unseen. I was somehow reassured by the presence of roadside monuments to car crash victims adorned with streaks of candle wax and ceremonial beer cans. For it meant that not all that died in these distant spots were abandoned and forgotten.

The liveliest things were springing jack rabbits, and they were friendly enough to distract me momentarily from the realities of the land. It was tranquil enough but being in the sun for so long and with so much daylight to go, it was easy to be unaware of the treacherous face the road and surrounding deserted land puts on when walking at night. With the light shining so brightly and being outside for so many hours it was difficult to imagine it at dark accompanied by the ruthlessness of night.

I was naive to initially think I was not vulnerable to weather, animals or some kind of human threat. Whenever I lost the rhythm in my step, I was worryingly suspicious of what human or animal might be hidden behind some patch of brush not far from my path. The more tired I became, the more I realized how vulnerable I was on this empty road to nearly anything that wanted to take a shot at me.

As quaint and restrained as Gaiman was, it was still an adjustment from the untouched land I had just spent a few hours walking through. A tiny place that came into being from the decision of a few who thought this would be a good place to start-over. Its setting could only be considered random. Gaiman was a peculiar, but boring little town behind a hill, near nothing.

The bust at the center of the town's little square, described by Chatwin remains, the only difference was its fresh markings of mediocre graffiti. Schoolchildren, among them more than a few with red hair and the palest of faces walked along the small sidewalks passed little tea shops whose signs were in Welsh, English and Spanish and emblazoned with some version of a Welsh dragon. One of the signs out front proclaimed to be rated best Tea House by the LA Times in 1997. The eight biting pages Chatwin had churned out now seemed like a miracle. There were hardly any people outside and less than a handful of shops open. No matter how Welsh the schoolchildren and teahouses looked, Gaiman was a disappointing town of people not Welsh enough and a random location seemingly picked out by some people too tired to continue walking further inland. Ethnicity took precedence over faith, for in Patagonia, towns of people had migrated across oceans not solely from large European countries like Italy and Spain but also from the continents' more obscure locations like Wales and Croatia. Red haired schoolchildren were proof enough that Welsh blood still flowed through the town.

On the entire walk, I thought of Gaiman as being an idyllic remote village where one could easily stay the rest of their life, looking like the distant villages in Wales with hills shaped like gumdrops sketched out first as a drawing. I was fully expecting the landscape around the town to look just like Wales, because Chinatowns always look like towns and cities in China. If the Chinese could do it, why not the Welsh?

My legs were shot after the long walk and the couple hours I wandered around the small town. There was little reason to stay and I felt satisfied in making the picture of Chatwin's eight pages more complete yet fooled by the strength of his prose that succeeded in making the town more interesting than its real-life form. All I had seen was land, dinosaurs and Welsh people, but I had trekked across the wide-open expanse of Patagonia that was more a thrill than any quirky town like Gaiman could be. I took the bus back to Trelew to rest my legs for two days.

****

There was nothing to see in the town of Rawson except for the pretty girl working behind the counter of a cafe disinterested in the men drinking stale coffee. Her long and deeply black hair was a hypnotic contrast to her light blue eyes. The men were all uneventful figures with disorderly facial hair and dirty baseball caps. The town was an orderly place with a disheveled bus station and a few cold and empty churches. There was a small square which all towns in Patagonia seem to have, with a couple statues of Generals and politicians. A large mural covered a long wall near a government building depicting the history of the conquest of the natives of Patagonia by European settlers. It was just another town to pass through that looks interesting after traveling even the small distance from Trelew. An hour-long bus ride between towns and cities in Patagonia always lasts longer in one's mind. The fact that these towns were there at all made them somewhat interesting, because that is always a relevant question with isolated places. Why is it there or rather, why is it still there? Once you arrive there is an inevitable disappointment with a place like Rawson. The disappointment of arrival. I wanted to see the ocean which was only a few more miles east.

As the shabby green local bus rumbled down an old open road towards the sea, Playa Rawson gradually grew larger and was like a temporary refugee camp at the edge of a desert that had existed for so long it became a real town. It was a place meant only for summer, but its residents were stuck there year-round. People out walking were ghostly and looked as though they had suddenly appeared. The empty streets and shoddy buildings gave the people an air of breaking a curfew imposed by some unseen occupying army. Those outside were dwarfed by the landscape surrounding the town and became the size of a small dried out bush. There was little reason to be on such streets, and most were making their way to the bus stop to head to Rawson and perhaps from there on to Trelew. It was winter and the town was largely empty save for a few stores selling vegetables, olive oil and cheap wine.

The only thing interesting in the town was the ocean that roared beside it and the sinister sky above which was the color of smeared cigar ashes. Any place along the ocean is pleasant no matter how somber, gloomy or bleak it may appear. One wonders why every stretch of beach is not framed by the ocean and homes of people admiring the view. Distant small dogs ran on the beach and appeared as though they were running in place. I didn't know whether they were running towards me or away from me. Huge waves broke just as a building would crumble onto streets and then glide more than a hundred yards up the beach, making it impossible to get close to the water. Far-off waves rose up then downwards like the distended stomach of a shapeless beast at rest and only broke in very shallow water near the shoreline. The ocean was an unwavering monster and each wave rolled out its shambolic tongue that changed color as it skated along the shore in every direction.

I sat in the sand immersed in cold wind that pleasantly changed the hue of my face to a reddish pink. The awesomeness of the ocean beside the endless shore of Patagonia was an entertainment and all man-made amusements became frivolous in comparison. There was a natural search for descriptions that drags and inevitably leads to a simple one such as, big, just as Montana is called the Big Sky State. There was little reason to look around for something worth discovering other than the sight of the ocean. It was more than enough. I was not just gazing out at the ocean but looking up at it, too.

When I swiveled my head back towards where I had seen the dog, it was gone. Within a few minutes there had been a change in scenery. Though the colors of the sky and the beach and the ocean were the same, the beach itself had become littered with whale carcasses. Large humpback whales, the kind one goes to see on tourist boats up near Puerto Madryn or off the coast of Alaska. At least a dozen of them now lay on the shore being soaked with the tail end of crashing waves as they slowly sank into the sand. Much further beyond the whales I thought I could see a few dogs heading towards the whales and me. But I was not sure, because they looked much bigger. They were growing much too fast as they closed the distance.

It was not dogs, but packs of dinosaurs coming down the beach to eat the whales. They moved faster the closer they got to the carcasses and nearly stumbled over one another reaching out for the first bites of fatty blubber. They took no notice of me. I was nothing compared to a whale. The large teeth thrashed into the now pathetically dead mammals. Their bodies were so lifeless it was as if they had never been alive. Gnawing off pieces like a lion would a Zebra. I thought this might be illusory thinking, but I was watching them. They were there. After all this was Patagonia. This is where dinosaurs are. Patagonia is where one sees dinosaurs. The sand around the whales was soaked in blood which the ocean quickly washed away, and the whale blubber and meat was covered in sand. They had rapidly devoured the immobile mammals and the carcasses and bones were left for the seagulls. The oversized ribs stood straight up and intact, as if untouched, because they had been eaten with swift efficiency. The once serene and deserted beach was now a scrapyard.

The sound of the birds overtook the thundering of the ocean for a few minutes and when the squawking subsided it meant the whales were completely gone and the murky feelings caused by their sudden absence was overtaken with the realization that their deaths were only natural in Patagonia. A Tyrannosaurus Rex rested beside me with its stomach and the bottom of its jaw evenly flat in the sand, the side of its body moving slowly with each long growling breath. Occasionally his tail swept a small wave of sand into the air. Young Velociraptors ran around the beach littered with the skeletons of whales like stripped cars in a junk yard. Most of the Velociraptors were wrestling and chasing each other into the ocean, proving to be weak swimmers when swept out further than they wished. One was a completely incompetent swimmer and quickly drowned in the melée making every creature present aware of its inability to compete with the powers of earth. This sudden death made each of the dinosaurs look vulnerable and less hard to believe they were born in the same manner as a chicken. The ocean was inarguably more menacing than the dinosaurs, even if it did not appear that way. We were all in two minds about the pleasures and beauty of the earth's landscape and its elements. Everything now seemed double-sided, the sand, the water, the sky, the trees, the rocks and we suspected such things to be deceitful and deceptive on the side we could not see. The ocean's natural beauty was deceiving, and we were all disappointed by nature's indifference to our being and even less to our suffering. But whether we sat on the beach or walked across the landscape to another distant town, we had little choice but to be at the mercy of nature.

7

Southern Patagonia

The colors of Patagonia shifted in a more winterly direction the further south I went. It was just about to be summer in New York and as the bus crossed into a colder climate below the equator, I realized this would be a year without a summer and a third winter awaited me after I returned home. In the previous couple of years I had become increasingly averse to the cold but the same difficulties of winter at home were exotic in a place as far away as Patagonia and I was less fussed about them. I did not have to make sure heaters worked or windows were properly sealed, they were someone else's worry. I was just passing through.

When I reached Comodoro Rivadavia I thought I would be able to spend the second half of the day walking around the city before catching the night bus further south to Rio Gallegos. After the sky had turned several shades of pink, I made my way back to the bus station, but the bus was delayed an hour and then another hour before it was canceled due to icy road conditions further south. There was little to do, even though the city was not small and nicely placed beside the Atlantic it felt like an outpost. The weight of the continent sitting beside it.

I was stuck for the night and forced to pass the time in a dull town. I was restless to push further south but found myself enjoying just how quiet the city was. It was a relief to not sleep on a bus again, blanketed by winter clothing and never fully asleep due to the rumbling engine. That night I slept better than I had in a long time and awoke unbothered that there was little to do in this town with a long name, for my body and spirit were composed, my mind quiet and content from the wintry air that blew into my ears. I wandered to the boatyards of the town and sat on the rocky shore in the sun like a runaway child. All around was rusted metal broken off of abandoned ships. I was forced to stop seeking for a while and being stuck turned traveling into a mental activity.

When I was back on the road, I sat on the top level of the bus at the front which had a large window giving a clear view of everything in front of us. The bus was the only noise in the hushed landscape, and for countless miles we drove towards skies with the most seductive shades of pink and purple, sometimes several shades of blue with a middle layer of pink.

****

Every traveler carries a degree of ignorance on each journey. I did my best to understand this sparsely populated land, but still the culture of Patagonia was fleeting - each person took on the character of someone passing through no matter how settled they were. Nationality was something that tended to fall by the wayside until you got up very close. After a short while, one learns to not search for such ornaments that belong in the 'old world,' and you approach everyone in a more basic and equal manner. Whether they were actually Argentinian or Chilean or from some distant place, they all took on the same ghostly character that had no imposing culture alongside it to confront visitors and wanderers with.

The people in and of Patagonia all belong to the Church of

Solitude. Visitors perhaps unknowingly, are a part of it, too. Even the most proud Argentine or Chilean of men cannot fully claim Patagonia as entirely a part of their country. For it is something all to itself, and until a large influx of people occurs it shall remain so. Solitude after all is a kind of belief system, and certainly a way of life for many which is so palpable in Patagonia that it begs the question, why is there not some sort of organized religion based upon it in Patagonia? But that question could easily be answered by saying that it is an unspoken religion that all naturally understand.

It is surprising that there has been no great religion to come out of Patagonia and equally so that there is no whole heartedly Patagonian religion, similar to say Mormonism. I had never heard of a particularly Patagonian religion or localized belief system, but there was a sense that something was missing from this empty and nearly desert like place. This made it unique to the rest of world, immune to the proclivities of humans to magnify superstition into full-fledged cults.

It was no hope of mine to find one, just a natural inclination to wonder of such things, for religions tend to come from such uninhabitable and difficult places. No great belief system, deep seated superstitions and subsequent cult has come out of this place. It is a place of dreams, exile and solitude rather than belief and superstition. People may be settled and tacked down so to speak, but systems of belief have not found a landing strip in Patagonia.

The American west is the next closest thing to Patagonia, but the creation of new belief systems has happened much more commonly, and it seems only natural for some sort of belief system or cultish creation to arise from this place where people so often live distant from the pressures and norms of long established societies. The Catholic Church has its place and Catholic is what most identify as, but the usual weight of its power and influence is not felt as strongly as in other places where it is established. Though Catholicism is a constant in

Argentina, and an impactful force, the ideology of the 'strongman' has come to be the real religion that has grown out of Argentine lands and most other countries on the continent, at times finding its way into Patagonia.

South America has always had plenty of megalomaniacal dictators, so absurd and brutal they take on the appearance of a caricature. Argentina has been ruled by several dictators, but notoriously during the middle of the 20th century was dominated by the presence of Juan Perón and his beloved wife Eva, better known to some as Evita.

The brutality of Perón's rule is widely known, and it existed for many years almost as an extension of European fascism, of Mussolini's Italy or Franco's Spain, and indeed came to be a refuge for Nazi's escaping the claws of justice in Europe. Strongmen like Perón naturally demanded a kind of worship and subservience and enforced such loyalty through the most brutal of methods. As Catholic as the continent is, dictators of both left and right, and some even with the unspoken backing of the Catholic Church transcended to an even greater power nearing idolatry. In that sense the religion of the continent has often become a kind of strong man totalitarianism. This natural inclination for the rise of such governments has arguably played a role in keeping down or stifling the growth of any kind of new spiritual belief system. Plus, it has allowed Patagonia to remain a sort of untouched slate where people of all beliefs, good and bad, can find refuge, being more or less left to themselves.

Ever since there have been Nazis, they seem to have reached every corner of the earth in one form or another. This is no less true of Patagonia. They are like cockroaches and they tend to find a way to survive one way or another. These sympathetic dictatorships in South America lent a hand to those fugitives of the Third Reich. The dictators, mostly of Argentina, but Chile, too, did a great deal of suppressing dissent and maintaining their grip on power through the nastiest of methods but they also took it upon themselves to protect and hide their fellow fascists escaping the web of justice that quickly succeeded their defeat in Europe. Soldiers, bureaucrats, doctors and sympathizers of all kinds quickly fled across the ocean to proverbial safety and freedom, all with the collusion of South American dictators and lower level contacts sympathetic to their lost cause. Nazis were not the first unseemly characters to find haven and hideout in the wilds of Patagonia.

Butch Cassidy and the Sundance Kid's flight from the United States is a well-known Patagonian story that ultimately ended in a bank robbery in Bolivia. Though, along with Butch's wife the trio successfully hid out in the northwestern part of Patagonia near El Bolsón and Esquel for a number of years, receiving inquiring looks from some locals before being stricken with the desire at pulling off another robbery in Bolivia. The story ultimately ends in mystery for no one really knows whether they were killed or successfully lived out the rest of their days in secret.

Though there may be more criminals and bank robbers similar to Butch and Sundance, the twentieth century Patagonian fugitive has been notoriously dominated by the unknown number of Nazis. Most notable of these fugitives is Adolf Eichmann, who lived for more than a decade in exile in a Buenos Aires suburb as a mechanic, before Nazi hunters and the Israeli government caught and smuggled him to Israel for a kind of symbolic trial against the whole of the Nazi regime. Hannah Arendt's book, *Eichmann in Jerusalem*, covers the trial in full and from Eichmann's testimony she coined the phrase the 'banality of evil,' which was due to Eichmann's reasoning for doing what he had done, being that he was just doing his job and complying with the commands of his superiors. The Israelis had no sympathy for this reasoning, and Eichmann was ultimately convicted. He is still the only person in Israel to be sentenced to death.

Whatever success Nazi hunters did have in the decades after the war they would never be entirely successful in rounding up all the Nazis that had fled to South America. There came to be a vast network of former Nazis and their subsequent descendants throughout the continent. This is known because in the following decades more Nazis, though in smaller numbers, would be outed and sometimes extradited to Europe for trial. The most recent case of a Nazi defector to come to light was that of Eric Priebke, who had lived more or less a private life in and around Esquel for over fifty years. He was found guilty of a massacre in Italy during the war and through a series of diplomatic maneuvers he was successfully extradited to Italy to stand trial.

I assumed it would be easy to come across these émigrés and their new families, to be able to observe them and call them out. But it was difficult to know where to start, after all, they were people in hiding and intended to stay that way. It was somewhat exciting to think I could come across such evil people in such a seemingly random place and expose them. But there was little hope of finding anything or anyone because Nazis in hiding do not go around telling random strangers that they are Nazis in hiding. All I could really do was look at the evidence of them being in Patagonia and to get a sense of their cruel presence, in the place they found refuge. If they were there they were certainly in their late eighties by now – but many of them undoubtably started families and their descendants were there, too. They were the legacy of both a crime and a continued secret. Crimes known by all the world and secrets known to only a few cagey communities on this most quiet of continents. One need not find Nazis in South America to come to a conclusion about Nazis in South America. Somehow Arendt's term of the 'banality of evil,' took on a different form when considering their presence there, but its meaning is all the more pungent with regards to the unfound fugitives. They lived among the citizens of numerous Latin American countries. Those who had fled the claws of justice were one thing, easily defined, but many of these defectors had started families with spouses perhaps unaware of their partner's past, and had children. What are the children of such people supposed to think of parents who have been fugitives for such heinous acts? A shameful secret, that will likely continue as such for numerous people.

Even though it may be a stealth presence there has also always been a presence of Jews in this distant land. I once attended a dinner in Israel and amongst the guests were two sisters hailing from Uruguay, whose family had fled Poland before the Holocaust commenced. Like many Jews in South America and elsewhere they could be said to have fled to Israel a couple decades ago, for the dual purpose of being a part of a Jewish homeland and also to escape the little more than anti-Semitic governments of South America's southerly countries. Though the sisters and their family were in less danger in Uruguay than their fellow Jews across the Rio de la Plata, their settling in Israel was a continuing sign to me of the hostility towards Jews in the region.

One of the most notable South American Jews of the literary sort was Jacobo Timerman. Born in Ukraine, his family emigrated to Argentina when he was a young boy, where later on Timerman was to become a well-known journalist in Buenos Aires. He was one of the many targets and victims of the regime in the 1970's. Timerman wrote four books, each of them displaying a deep devotion to anti-authoritarianism. Of the four books, his first, written in his fifties, 'Prisoner without a Name, Cell Without a Number' chronicled his arrest, imprisonment and subsequent torture by the Videla regime. There is perhaps no better first-hand account, certainly none more eloquent, of the dirty work of the so called 'dirty war' that went on for years in Argentina. Thousands of people were kidnapped and never seen from again, and soon were collectively given the ghostly description of los desaparecidos, 'the disappeared.' In several towns in Patagonia and not far from Buenos Aires there are sometimes strings stretching across pedestrian streets with headshot photos dangling like miniature flags of people who were kidnapped and never seen from again.

Seeing all of the photos reminded me of Timerman's gripping story, who also had disappeared for a time, but was thankfully released and able to tell his story through his beautiful writing. Not only does Timerman describe the cruelty and unmerciful actions of his torturers and their employers, he vividly describes the overbearing anti-Semitism that was unashamedly spewed in his direction, towards other Jewish prisoners and world Jewry en masse.

It was so prevalent in the minds of his torturers that during and between torture sessions they would condemn Timerman and world Jewry for the world's ills including, the results of Freudian theory on Christian family values, the supposed controlling of world banking systems by Jewish families and communities, followed by the promulgation of communism by Marx and Bolshevism by Russian Jews. Not only was Timerman faced with countless blows from the baton and electric shocks he was constantly given an undermining reason why he and his fellow Jews were also deserving of such treatment.

After spending at least a month in Patagonia, I really started to get a sense of the immensity of its size, and just how uninhabited it really was. It was a place that would take decades if not centuries to populate were some foreign power ever interested in seeking to conquer it from the Argentines and Chileans. It would take a concerted effort backed by a significant military force.

This is why the typical paranoia and exaggeration that infects the most anti-Semitic brutes was no more present than in the claim they threw at Timerman, that Jews were plotting to take over Patagonia.

This was perhaps a prevalent worry for a regime that colluded with Nazis to give them safe haven, most notably in distant Patagonia.

Timerman's account is believable but difficult to get through and withstand for its graphic and horrifying scenes. His suffering is terrible and only made more vivid and nasty through his concise prose. His account stayed with me and was difficult to forget. I had finished it halfway through traveling across Patagonia and thus I saw this empty landscape with two sets of eyes. The claim that Jews were plotting to take Patagonia was perhaps the most horrifying aspect of the book, even beyond the torture Timerman suffered. The violence of such a regime almost too easy to understand and condemn. The breadth of Patagonia sat in front of me and its distances were nearly immeasurable, and it had taken me days to get across overland. The absurdity of the claim at first made me laugh, but I slowly realized just how wicked it was and it mirrored nearly every other conspiracy aimed at Jews before and after World War II.

As a writer Timerman was anti-authoritarian wherever he found himself. After moving to Israel and spending a number of years there, he rejected the government's war in Lebanon in 1982. Deeming General Sharon to be guilty of committing atrocities against the citizens in southern Lebanon. He later traveled in Chile to document the stories from the families of victims of the Pinochet regime. His final book, *Cuba: A Journey*, was a survey of the Castro regime's failure to bring any kind of prosperity to the island and the suffering it inflicted on its people. After some years in Israel, he returned to Argentina where he lived out the rest of days writing in the same vein as he had always done. His writing was complete and his words live on, and therefore so do the others that are still 'disappeared.'

8

Punta Arenas and the Strait of Magellan

I was exhilarated to be in Punta Arenas, for it was my halfway point and the final frontier of the Western world. I considered it and not Ushuaia as a pinnacle, because it was still a part of the continent, whereas Tierra del Fuego and its largest city were an island unto itself. Punta Arenas was a place to turn around from and travel an entirely different direction than the one I had been traveling for so many miles. It was the end of going south for there was really nowhere else to go. Antarctica is an oblivion, a great nothing and should it melt it would be even less. Arriving in Punta Arenas after dozens of hours on buses through empty landscapes was like arriving at home to a place just as quiet as those empty fields and mountains I admired through the windows. There was a palpable connection between it and the rest of the continent. From the ledge of the city there was a perspective of the whole of the continent and even further north to the rest of Latin America. This was its conclusion and more dramatically a culmination of Latin culture. Whether it started in Miami, Tijuana or Havana, the final stopping point and the place where I was to turn around was perched at the edge of the Strait of Magellan. During the week I was in and around Punta Arenas, I found myself whispering to myself the name of that seemingly ancient explorer. It was on books and t-shirts, and this part of Patagonia was happily known as the Land of Magellan. A fact which never ceased to please me.

I was relieved to be there, for I had made it through all those miles unscathed and further relieved to find a city filled with infinite solitude on arrival. I looked at the few walkers in the streets and the small homes and quiet apartment buildings that were the dwellings of people who were experiencing this kind of peace for their entire lives. The Strait itself and much of the land it passes alongside is untouched as though it has not been discovered, not been conquered at all and still not claimed by any country. Magellan and his crew of two hundred and fifty passed through the Strait hundreds of years before on a treacherous journey in an effort to circumnavigate the globe with what was considered advanced technology in their day, but today appears primitive.

In and around Punta Arenas, idling is an inevitable activity accompanied by gazing out at the Strait. There was a regular feeling of relief in all manner of things. The simplest of walks on the flattest of roads along the Strait were as satisfying as a trek through a mountainous landscape. Along its shores there was the occasional fisherman stood far away on a sand bar rarely catching anything. The skies were perpetually filled with clouds but reflected sharply off the water's surface. A few feet above the water flocks of birds flew in a long straight line behind one another, which only made the Strait a soothing and more peaceful place.

When I left I felt I was always leaving from Punta Arenas and for most every mile I went in a southerly direction I was always heading towards Punta Arenas and with every mile there was a bubbling anticipation, a hopefulness and happiness that one can travel this far of a distance and still be greeted by such a beautiful place with pleasant and welcoming people. The presence of young soldiers walking in threes around the city, adorned with fur hats was an odd reminder that even the remotest parts of the earth are important enough for nations to fight over. There is a full-scale training base in the city and the rowdy young soldiers from all parts of the country are restless to be elsewhere.

It was nearly impossible to fully absorb the size of the Strait and the daring voyage that Magellan took. Magellan's journey was the culmination of a fruitful career as a soldier and explorer first in the service of his home country Portugal, and then in the service of Spain. After many years faithfully serving the Portuguese King in the east during which he was badly wounded, he returned home to virtually no welcome. Restless and bored with life at home in a Portugal that was reaping the benefits of a flourishing trade in spices, slaves, and jewels, he developed plans to find a new route to the east in the direction Columbus had tried. Columbus had incorrectly thought he had reached the East, but by the time Magellan had set out it was determined that these lands were indeed 'New' and not an extension or westerly part of Eastern Asiatic lands. The desire for new and better routes to the East thrived because of European desire for the goods and flavors of the East. It was also making seafaring nations and its entrepreneurs and explorers unbelievably rich. European nations had also grown tired at the difficulties and hindrances brought on by the virtual blockade that was Muslim territories which forced them to pay crippling tariffs in order to pass through. The only other option being the long and arduous journey around the whole of Africa and across the Indian ocean.

A man named Francisco Serrão was a dear friend of Magellan's and fought alongside him in numerous battles in the East, including one in which Magellan saved his life during a battle at Malacca. They remained blood brothers until their deaths which happened less than a year apart only a few hundred miles from each other. After Magellan had returned to Portugal and Serrão had settled in the East, the two kept in regular contact. It was Serrão's regular talk of the Spice Islands in modern day Indonesia that continually inspired Magellan to seek a new route to get there.

After finding no support from his King or country, he renounced his citizenship and took on the arduous process of lobbying the Spanish King with the help of some interested and friendly Spaniards and other Portuguese adventurous types who had found more faith and interest in their expeditious plans from the Spanish ruling classes.

Magellan declared that he knew the actual route to the east before he had even traveled it, which made it seem that he knew someone that had already done it or had some unique information about how to do it. He had set his sights on this route to circumnavigate the globe based on a false map and would end up the discoverer of the actual route. Magellan had access to a map that was made by Martin Behaim, who never visited the Americas, but compiled information collected from other Portuguese sailors navigating the coast of South America.

The Portuguese sailors never went completely into the Rio de la Plata and thus never found a path to the Pacific. He and his fellow map makers were given information that the indentation in the continent leading to the Strait was actually the indentation at the Rio de la Plata twelve degrees in latitude further north. Behaim had never crossed the Atlantic to see the mouth of the Rio de la Plata, thus it was thought that the mouth of the Rio de la Plata was the southernmost point of the continent. Magellan had acted on an honest mistake and ended up discovering the actual route to the Pacific.

Had the information been correct, the expedition would likely have seemed much more arduous and perhaps not been approved by the Spanish Kings. It was Magellan's passion for the unknown that spurred this journey, his discovery of the Strait and the true size of the planet's circumference. All because of a mistake.

The fortitude of Magellan's character would change history after his fleet reached the Rio de la Plata and he directed his crew further south into entirely uncharted waters. Slowly, the fleet sailed down the coast of the continent, investigating every indentation in the land, gradually sewing suspicion in some of the crew as to whether or not he knew the route he had said he did. These waters were rough and that meant calling into port at the bay of present-day Puerto San Julian, which was surrounded by a most desolate landscape. On my way down the coast in the bus, there was little in sight to inspire a different description. It was a place that quickly lowered the men's spirits. It was during this time that Magellan and his men would give this part of the continent the name of Patagonia after they had sighted a large creature whom they called Patagão, 'big foot.' It was a man who was exceptionally larger than any man the European crew had ever seen. At first they thought he was some sort of monstrous creature, but it was in actuality a man with gigantism, but also with quite primitive instincts for they watched the man grab rats off the ground and bite into them while still alive.

When they pushed south Magellan was forced to brutally quell a mutiny by some of the Spanish crew suspicious of his motives. The journey was not even halfway through and Magellan and his men were constantly moving in unknown territory. With such adversity and uncertainty most men would have turned back or succumbed to the treachery of such a mission, but Magellan's stubbornness was useful. He was obsessed with the idea of a hidden strait and on October 21st, 1520 his obsession would be realized. This was the first ever fleet of ships to sail into these waters. They turned into an indentation thinking it was a kind of canal but upon getting much further down they found the water still tasted of salt. It was undeniable that there was an ocean at the other side.

For nearly six weeks they sailed through the Strait into various dead-end bays and coves, eventually finding their way to the Pacific, which Magellan named for its nearly constant pacifying colors and calmness. The days I spent beside the Strait were as peaceful and serene as any other I had ever experienced. Days of idling were an inevitability in such a place, for the opportunity to gaze upon some of the most beautiful and bountiful settings were ever present. All the walks I had taken, a few miles in each direction along the Strait, made me admire the daring and awesomeness of what Magellan had achieved.

As still as the waters of the Strait appear it was and often can still be a treacherous place to navigate. Magellan spent six weeks traversing its bays and shallow shores. I stared out to the still waters and its surroundings in awe of its immensity. It was a majestic place under almost always cloudy skies just as they had been when Magellan first set eyes on it. As much as I looked, there was little entertainment to find in the city of Punta Arenas. There were families and churchgoers and small business owners and all matters of life moving with a collective ease. The city was like much of the rest of Patagonia, quiet and wishing little else than to be. I gradually thought the same for myself. There was no reason to look for anything other than nature and each day as I walked further down the shores of the Strait, it became evident that it was a high entertainment to be present under the gloomy skies of the Strait of Magellan. Something told me to come here, but I cannot put it down to an exact phrase – perhaps it was something as superficial as its place on the map, perhaps it was the audacity of Magellan's journey. It was a place whose history was peculiar to me. It is a history common to that of many parts of the New World, difficult, dangerous, and fraught with violence between immigrants and natives, where fortunes were made and lives were lost. There has been much life in the Land of Magellan, but it is so quiet and so peaceful it still feels undiscovered. Even up close it is a mystery.

9

Andrea

The poster in the Bariloche bus station said the best hotel in all of Argentina was only a few miles away. A large building was set dramatically on a hill surrounded by lakes and snow-capped mountains as though it were once a country estate built for a robber baron. It was luxurious, secluded and a possible setting for a sequel to The Shining. It seemed like the perfect place to hide or at least feel like you were hiding. Its funny name, Hotel Llao Llao, and mountainous surroundings gave it an air of being the only hotel of a miniature European principality where the sole business is banking, and adventurous day-trippers get their passports stamped at the post office for fun. The local bus passed by the little town of Colonia Suiza, named as such for the Swiss immigrants that had settled there decades before. A small uneventful place where chocolates and souvenirs emblazoned with Swiss flags are sold for similar prices. Leaving Bariloche and driving beside the lakes, the road was darkened from the shadows of trees and it felt like crossing an unofficial border meant only for locals. The hotel was even larger than it appeared in the picture and the setting more beautiful with the sky turning pink and gold from the sun that was falling into the lake.

There were few guests with the exception of some wealthy

Argentine families and couples being served afternoon tea by waiters in gold vests in the main lobby fit with antler chandeliers. Above the log cabin paneling of the empty hallways there were photographs of Eisenhower during his visit as well as other former heads of state but with less familiar faces. Views of the lakes and mountains could be had from almost every window. Lining the main floor were rooms reserved for reading, gathering, watching television - but all were left empty. A pale faced yet pretty Argentine girl worked the lonely gift shop. The insides of her cheeks making sensual noises every time she moved. A grand patio in the back of the hotel looked out to the lake and Colonia Suiza in the distance. It was the setting for countless weddings and parties, but now it was winter and though there was no snow on the ground, it was cool enough to keep the guests inside and grand ceremonies in warmer locations. I bundled up and had the patio to myself for a couple days, bathing my face and bare feet in the cool air that swept up from the lake, writing letters, reading, smoking cigars and drinking all kinds of coffee and tea.

After a couple days on the patio I walked along the lakes to where a few of the trails began into the Llao Llao Park hoping to get lost for most of the day in the woods and climb to the peak of the little Cerro Llao Llao for a view of the surrounding lakes and mountains. It was a chance to be even more secluded. An empty golf course spoiled the land around the hotel and a few little houses had aggressive German Shepherds clawing and barking into the fences that they paced alongside of. The trees grew denser and the road darkened even though it was mid-morning. When I got to a gap in the trees and the beginning of a path at the edge of a carless road there was a small box of a ranger station. Inside a woman heard my footsteps and came out to offer some advice. When she said her name was Andrea I was not convinced. It came off as a carelessly chosen pseudonym, but I did not reveal my suspicions. Strikingly beautiful and in her late forties with unkempt blonde hair, she was nearly six feet tall and dressed as if she would be modeling for an outdoor apparel catalogue. The accent was not that of an Argentine, in fact it threw me at first, but I could tell she was from somewhere east of Prague. Her expression was rather blank, and her eyes stared softly into the distance giving her the appearance of someone in constant reflection. She wanted to do all the talking and did so slowly while pointing out a few routes to take through the park, where to go and what to avoid, on a little fold-out map.

We both laughed instantly when she guessed I was from Australia.

"I always guess Australia when someone speaks English." It became more obvious she was not an Argentine, but I could not figure out exactly where she was from. I asked her more questions just to listen to her accent.

Until I finally asked.

"Yugoslavia," she quickly said, not wanting to reveal anymore. I had been leaning towards Slovakia.

It was a peculiar thing to say considering that Yugoslavia is no longer a country and had been broken up into several countries for nearly twenty years. She tried to guard herself from where the simple question she had also asked me might lead to. I did not feel too out of line thinking it was only natural to be made curious if someone similarly said they were from Tanganyika, Siam, or Northern Rhodesia. She knew it was something that most people would just accept, not noticing the decoy. But she said it as if it were perfectly natural to call it by that dated and discarded name. In a way, she was stuck there, and she believed it. That's what it was called for her.

I was drawn to her and wanted to know more. I thought of other older women I had met and how guarded they were because of their looks, but Andrea was graceful and tired of the frivolous matter of her own beauty. There was something else she was on guard about. Every question I asked or thought of came off more intrusive than the last and she was becoming visibly unsettled, but too polite and reserved to say so. All she wanted was to be helpful and her answers shortened with each question.

She continued to talk, but still in a monotone in order to control the conversation. I was determined to know which country she was from and interrupted her in order to find out.

"Where I come from it does not matter what country you are from, only the blood in you is what matters."

I knew what she was getting at, but I wanted her to say a place other than Yugoslavia.

"Which city, then?"

She broke her casual stare, turned her face square to mine with an offended look, then after a few dragging seconds, said, "Belgrade." The pausing look she gave turned the surrounding mass of trees into a sea of spectators. The sound of rustling leaves was like someone coughing in a quiet crowded theater and all the spaces in between the trees were now darker.

That city and her mention of blood was all one needed to know to understand the unchanging look on her face. It was the expression of a person who was incapable of forgetting the things she had seen. Her stare was more than a cue to stay off the subject, but a way of making me see what she could not stop seeing. I did not press her anymore and repeated a few questions about which paths to take into the park.

I had met a few refugees or relatives of refugees from the Yugoslav wars and they had always been upbeat and happy to be living in America, satisfied with the distance from their country. The war had ended for them. But for Andrea, it was something that was very much in front of her, even the mentioning of the country brought too much to mind. She was as far as one could be from the Balkans but for her it became ever present with the questions of a nosey passerby.

I gave up knowing I would likely see her on my way back and set off. As I walked through the woods, the tranquility of the park put Andrea and nearly everything else to the back of my mind. At the top of Cerro Llao Llao it felt like a window into Switzerland. The lush beauty of the park was surreal, and I wondered whether I was in Argentina or some obscure Alpine outpost.

I rested beside a small secluded lake surrounded by mountains and woods with only a small path and a dock at the end jutting out a few feet into the still water. The paths were so dense at times that my eyes could not focus, making all the trees and bushes blend together, creating a blur of brown and green. At times it was so dense that it almost completely blocked the sunlight, which poked through in narrow streaks, making it both dark and cold. Steppingstones made out of tree trunks had been placed in large puddles that had flooded parts of the trail and other times it was necessary to climb over massive trees that had fallen across the small paths. A few Roman bridges were built in order to cross steep gullies with creeks running underneath. The bridges were pretty and well-built and made it feel as though I were trespassing on a country estate.

Having marched around for nearly seven hours I found myself back where I started and walked by the little cabin noticing Andrea still reading the map of the park. I wanted to talk to her some more but knew she did not want to be bothered. I even thought of inviting her to dinner, but the more I thought of it I realized there was nothing left to say. The way simple questions unsettled her was unsettling to me. The wall was too high to climb. She wanted to be left alone and participate only when helping others. As I walked down the road towards the hotel, I realized Andrea was hiding.

She was hidden more or less in plain sight, and in fact could easily be found. It was not as if anyone was looking for a Serbian immigrant in Llao Llao, Argentina, but there was a contentedness and confidence in her that knew nobody would ever think to look for her there.

Nothing from her old life would be able to find her. Yugoslavia was another planet and in fact, no longer existed. She had found a remote place where people for the most part did not ask questions and were not concerned with the past or even who you were. More importantly it was a place where blood was of no importance. Later that night, as I settled down on the back patio of the hotel I wondered if Andrea had seen that same poster in the bus station.

10

Neruda and Central Chile

Stretches of open grass, rows of vineyards and snowcapped maps eventually turned into a large city. I was sat on the only train line in Chile, which started in Chillán and ended in Santiago. I wondered why there was not a train line from one end of the country to the other. It would be more or less a straight line for two thousand miles. Trains are a pleasant way to get around and through lush landscape such as the vineyards surrounding Santiago, the laboriousness of travel is gone, and you float through the countryside. I could feel the city's pulse before I even arrived. There was a gradual haze to the air and the inevitable pollution of a city. I arrived at the station and walked for an hour down the long boulevard that stretches across the center of the city. While I momentarily paused at several stop lights awaiting the noisy traffic to pass I was somewhat awestruck by the sight of snowcapped mountains monumentally set behind the city.

The first thing I did in Santiago was try to buy a plane ticket for Easter Island. It was a place that had been on my mind for as long as I could remember, and whenever someone asked where I wanted to go if I could go anywhere, my answer was always Easter Island. I was gradually making my way there, and the last step was the long flight across the ocean. I was a excited when I got to the little ticketing agency near the Plaza de Armas, but quickly found that this being the busiest season, there was not a flight for almost two weeks. So I pushed it out even further, and bought a ticket for when I got back from Valparaíso. Despite being delayed a little longer to go to Easter Island, I was still happy being in Santiago. Knowing when my flight was I knew I had a good amount of time to hang out in both Santiago and Valparaíso. My plan was to spend a week on Easter Island, and once back in Santiago I would make my way up the coast of Chile and into Peru.

The Plaza de Armas was a jovial place, and all its busy pedestrian streets leading to it felt much like the center of Buenos Aires. Being that I had not been in a large city since Buenos Aires for nearly two months it was a pleasure to be amongst the pulse of a city once again. One of the first scenes I saw was a man and a woman arguing, which culminated with the woman hitting the man over the head with a Styrofoam basket full of French Fries. She then ran off and looked back scared as the man slowly followed.

Santiago is a wide-ranging city that stretches across the center of the country for miles. Much of it looks prosperous and the parts that do not are not particularly menacing. It is a capital that encapsulates the entire country and its location in the center of the country is literally a crossroads for any traveler.

I walked around till late, watched a wedding in the main cathedral and found an old restaurant that had the feel of a social club, just before it was closing. With waiters in bow tie, it reminded me of how I had done the same in Buenos Aires. Stopping in a city with so much to see and so many people to meet and talk to I realized I was living a nomadic existence. It was nice to know I would be in one place more or less a couple of weeks. Santiago is so welcoming and agreeable that there is no such thing as a foreigner. In parts it is filled with leisure which stifles nearly all of one's inquisitiveness. You can quickly become a local in a city as big as Santiago. There was no real mystery to be uncovered. The only thing to do was get to Neruda's house.

I had no real plan other than to wander the city like I would any other and talk to whomever was willing. However, one thing I was eager to know more about was Pablo Neruda. In Chile, it is difficult not to notice the almost spiritual presence of Neruda. He is easily and often felt in Chilean society not simply for being a Nobel Prize winning poet, but because he is memorialized in murals on the walls of buildings across Chile and is a political symbol for much of the political Left in Latin America, made evident at political rallies and in daily conversation. His presence is more tangible than the usual artistic and political martyr, because his three houses still stand and are considered something like places of pilgrimage for his admirers. They are a window into the country itself for curious travelers and passersby.

I found myself standing in front of each of Neruda's houses eager to see what was inside. I had never been in the house of a poet, let alone three of them. Poets are decidedly different and eccentric souls, but Neruda is an altogether unique character among his fellow poets. In Santiago, La Chascona is nearly unavoidable as it sits in the youthful Bellavista neighborhood, making it nearly impossible not to take a look inside.

A quaint pedestrian street in a nice bohemian neighborhood is the setting of Neruda's central Santiago residence. In front of the house a small amphitheater is built into the incline of the street, which helps frame the house as a stage. Built into the side of a hill, the house is as quirky in its design as it is in the cluttered decor that are the souvenirs and furnishings of Neruda's travels. Its sea blue color is simply reminiscent of Neruda's love of the sea. The house was built more for his secret lover, Matilde, who would become his third wife. Initially a place to rendezvous and hide out from his second wife, Delia. Both relationships carried on for some years, one physical, the other platonic in nature, coming to an end when Delia found out the true nature of the relationship, she eventually had enough.

There were plenty secret compartments, narrow doors, passageways, and oddly placed windows. From the street its size is deceiving, but even with a pretty center courtyard it never feels grand. Most of the rooms are small and require turning one's body to maneuver through especially with the abundance of furniture and artifacts. La Chascona feels as though a child designed his own life-size playhouse or urban treehouse. The knick-knacks and trinkets, quirky furniture that line every wall and corner made the house look more like a playroom than the home of one of the world's most accomplished poets.

It is remarkable that the house still stands, because it was sacked and burned during the 1973 coup that led to the downfall of President Allende which was shortly followed by the death of Neruda himself. Without La Chascona there is no museum devoted to Neruda in Chile's capital.

Even with all the possessions that cover the entire house, it did not feel like it belonged to him. Neruda's presence was not entirely there which is fitting for he did not spend all of his time there, and it was more of a love nest. This did not surprise me for it is difficult for any urban home to retain the aura of its owner, because cities have a tendency to give any home or apartment the aura of a hotel room. The house looked inward and everything was geared to the inside like any good urban hide out, unlike Neruda's two other houses.

The souvenirs and furniture that littered every possible spot made it resemble a storage space and it had all come from a much larger home. I was certain that La Chascona did not give a full picture of the man, but it was a fitting introduction to the other side of Neruda's life. Which often involved hiding as a result of his politics as well as his double love life.

The house is a fun view into the mind of man who spent much of his day scribbling down the prettiest thoughts into long and short verse. But afterwards, I was left wanting to know more about Neruda. I had read more than a few of his great poems, my favorite being Love Sonnet XVII.

I was certain there was a great deal more to know about a man who could write such beautiful lines of verse. Surely, he was not just merely a writer. It is a frustrating paradox to find that the creator of such romantic verse was an unapologetic supporter of Josef Stalin.

Neruda lived an unquestionably political life. More so than even some politicians and perhaps his poetry overshadows that, but to the wider world it is lesser known just how much of Neruda's daily life was tied up in Chilean and world politics. This can be said of a lot of artists and of course non-artists of his time. Neruda's life spanned three quarters of the 20th century and his was an almost quintessentially twentieth century life that was inevitably wrapped up in two world wars, the Spanish Civil War and for much of the last half of his life, the Cold War. His death along with that of President Salvador Allende's tied the two men together as martyrs for one small battleground of the struggle between the United States and the USSR.

During his twenties he was a restless traveler and would remain so for much of his life, setting off for five years serving in diplomatic positions for Chile in Burma and Sri Lanka (then Ceylon), Batavia (Java, Indonesia), and Singapore. He would later serve in diplomatic posts in Mexico and as his fame grew and opportunities opened in Spain and France. The 1930's was an equally active decade for Neruda as his travels continued, but during his time at home he was faced with a population like many other South American countries that had a significant amount of German immigrants and thus many loyal supporters of Germany's newly elected Führer. One time, in a small Chilean enclave with an overwhelmingly German population he was forced to give a Nazi salute to a picture of Hitler in order to use a payphone. The presence of fascism was plain to see and on the rise in Neruda's world, as it was elsewhere, making it almost impossible not to choose a side or develop strong beliefs one way or the other. But the great event that shaped the political beliefs of so many artists and non-combatants was the Spanish Civil War. Spain was a testing ground for both Hitler and Stalin, which forced Neruda, like so many other famed artists, to take a stand with the 'Republicans' against the fascist leader Francisco Franco who welcomed Hitler's support. The war was covered by the great men and women of letters of the day, Hemingway, Dos Passos, Gellhorn, and there was Orwell who took up arms in the Lenin Brigade, surviving a bullet to the neck. Federico Garcia Lorca, the Spanish poet was famously an early victim of the fascist revolt and subsequently reached the symbolic status of a martyr for much of Republican Spain. Neruda did not go so far as to get in the trenches but by spending time in Spain during some of the earliest fighting he was close to the war and made his presence felt in the way that a writer would. Neruda did his most as a propagandist for the cause, but his most remembered contribution during the war was the organization and shipping of over two hundred Spanish refugees to Chile on a freighter. Many of whom lived to thank him many years later, still as residents of their new country, Chile.

Spain was the intersection of world politics in the 1930's. With so many sides and factions there was seemingly no correct side to choose. Every side had its drawbacks and there was little option but for the nastiest and most ruthless goes the spoils. The fascists were obviously evil and the collected opposition was a slowly fracturing mess as a result of hysteria over who carried a purer form of leftist belief. A reality portrayed vividly in Orwell's, *Homage to Catalonia*. The fighting in Spain would come to have consequences for the rest of the world and what happened there was certainly watched closely. Spain being the eternal mother country of Spanish America, Neruda was keen to put down a stake in the fight. It was not difficult for the citizens of Latin America to be drawn to pick sides in this war and for a man like Neruda, it was inevitable.

Two beautiful speeches survive in a collection of Neruda's nonfiction writings, *Passions and Impressions,* that are evident of some of his most passionate political writing, naturally laced with his talent for putting life and emotion beautifully into words. One was a eulogy delivered in Paris in 1937 for Federico Garcia Lorca in which he condemned the Franco regime, and went on to say that he and his fellow poets of Spanish America and Spain should never forgive Lorca's killers. Many years later he had not forgotten Lorca nor the war in Spain because in a speech entitled, '*They Try to Extinguish the Light of Spain,*' delivered in 1968 in São Pãulo upon the dedication of a monument to the memory of Federico Garcia Lorca, Neruda's passions for both art and politics were still beautifully intertwined more so than any political poem he ever wrote. The subjects of Lorca and the Spanish Civil War, thirty years later, remained ever present for him and still riled him to speak forcefully and of course eloquently, because Spain was still under the control of the Franco regime, the same regime that killed Lorca. It ends beautifully by saying that there would be no better monument to Lorca's memory than the liberation of Spain.

World events were not the only thing to shape his political beliefs. Though Neruda was a restless traveler, he did not have to travel far to experience the tumultuousness of politics. Often times politics found him, and politics in Chile molded Neruda just as much and he was never hesitant to delve into the politics of his home country.

Being a man who traveled so often throughout his life one wonders why a man with three houses was so often elsewhere. Many of his travels were not solely out of wanderlust but often the result of political exile. The changing hands of power in Chile, meant Neruda had to flee from his own country or go into hiding within Chile for some time. While serving as a Senator, the opposition party led by Gonzalez Videla came to power, and an arrest warrant was quickly put out for Neruda and he spent a year hiding throughout Chile with the help of friends. A year which ended with him escaping over the Andes Mountains on horseback to Argentina and ultimately fleeing to France. He did all this at the age of 46. But Videla did not stop the pursuit of Neruda at the borders of Chile. Even though there was a great distance between his exiled home and his country, Videla's government consistently kept up the pressure to have Neruda arrested or detained wherever he was in the world for the next four years. Thus, causing Neruda to hide within France and bounce around Europe and trips to politically sympathetic countries like Russia and China as well as a return to India.

****

The geography of Chile is unique. With one of the longest coastlines on one side and an endless stretch of mountains on the other, it gives the country a kind of seclusion rare for most countries. But what is most unique about Chile is how narrow its borders are from east to west and how far apart from north to south. At any spot in Chile it only takes an hour to leave the country, for the borders are never far. But to get from one end of the country to the other can take two or three days overland.

Before getting to Santiago I passed through a number of towns in Araucania province. In an effort to split up the long journey to Santiago stopping in a few uneventful towns along the way. I had traveled north towards Santiago, stopping in Temuco and Chillán. Temuco was as grey and rainy as Neruda always described it, but much more developed with its center littered with shopping centers and office buildings. I passed through the quiet city of Los Ángeles and regretted not making the detour to the coastal city of Concepcion, known for its earthquakes and leftist politics. It is a political stronghold of the communist party and all sorts of radical student movements have begun and continue to dominate the local political scene.

It was Temuco that most interested me, but there was little sign of Neruda. I started thinking more about the man in his childhood city. He lived there more than one hundred years before, and the city was undoubtedly larger and louder and riddled with the noises of cars and crowds. I was walking where he walked. And it made his memoirs more vivid as I read them. I knew that searching for signs of Neruda in Temuco was a lost cause, but I was happy both nights I spent in the city were rainy nights, in fact it never stopped raining. The experience of the raininess in Neruda's hometown was one of his most vivid memories that stayed with him until his last days when describing them in his memoirs. Neruda often spoke of his most vivid childhood memory being his wet socks and his cold feet. Leaving his shoes out to dry near the fire after walking home in the rain. So many other children would have had a similar experience, I thought.

In Santiago I caught up on messaging people back home and read a whole biography of Neruda, and as much of his poetry as I could in between. The World Cup was what most people were interested in, and in and around Bellavista the bars were filled with people from all countries wearing their nation's jersey or colors. Packs of German and Australian fans mixed with Argentineans, American and English fans. I went to the Beaux-Arts Museum and tried out the French restaurants in some of the more posh parts of town. On the eastern end of the city everyone gravitated to the massive new W. Hotel. It was a touch of Miami Beach in the middle of a city surrounded by mountains. It was hard to resist the scene and restaurants, the carefully manicured clothes and people that lunched on oysters, smoked large cigars and spoke of money and made deals.

****

After spending a week in Santiago, I had a great desire to see the coastal city of Valparaíso. It was a little more than an hour from Santiago to the coast which in my mind was an almost bafflingly short distance considering every ride I had taken north towards Santiago was at least eight hours. The geographical shape of Chile became more vivid for its extreme lengths were sharply contrasted with its narrow width.

I first stopped in Viña del Mar just north of Valparaíso. Much of the surrounding towns were small and very posh, more conservative seaside towns that resemble something like Palm Beach, Florida. Wealth is on display, the people are dressed well, nannies push strollers alongside well-manicured families, and many indulge in the seaside restaurants, sipping on champagne. The beaches are full and bustling with young people, talking to everyone as they move down the beach or relax and talk to those strolling. Pleasant and safe enough, and a good place to feel protected from all the world's ills.

I had no desire to stay and took the seaside train to Valparaíso. The sun shone brightly in both places, but Valparaíso had more life to it. Valparaíso is a charming city set beautifully on Chile's coast. One of its largest ports — the city wraps around the bay on which it is set. The city greets you firstly with the bay but then the lower part of the city arrives in blunt fashion with its three noisy boulevards threaded through each other. If Viña del Mar was a place of sophisticated maturity then Valparaíso was a rebellious teenager, colorful, full of artists and working-class people.

Any place built into the side of a hill and with many steep inclines would naturally build character in its people and the city itself. To be faced with such hills looks a daunting obstacle for the newcomer. A place that is in sight and seemingly within walking distance can take half an hour or more to reach if the route is not carefully planned. There are steep winding staircases carved into the hills snaking their way up and down.

Walking is difficult because of the hills but made easier with the playful sight and efficient use of 'funiculars,' elevators that are built into the side of hills. You can quickly slide up and down for a few pesetas, minimizing the steep walking one would have to do in either direction. Painted in bright colors, the funiculars look like a carnival ride rather than a form of transportation. The city takes on a different face up in the hills, much quieter and at rest. It costs something like a quarter for each ride, but I wanted to trek up to Neruda's house, La Sebastiana, set nearly at the top of the hill where the streets begin to flatten out.

From the flat main streets of Errazuriz and Blanco and Brasil that hug tightly to the bay a mere one-mile walk was made much more arduous by the steep hills that ascend to the top. It would be odd for Neruda to not have a house in Valparaíso. It is a poetic city hard to avoid and gives no reason to resist and is perfect for a man like Neruda. It was only fitting that Neruda should have a house in Valparaíso, for it is a city difficult to not feel attached to. A place that perhaps appreciates him more so than the capital.

There are more than a few murals dedicated to Neruda's memory emblazoned on the sides of buildings. Though, much of his time was not spent in Valparaíso. With all his traveling and two other houses, including his beloved Isla Negra an hour south, La Sebastiana was a place of sporadic escapes. Also, another place, like La Chascona, filled with his treasures from his travels abroad. There are maps and murals and plenty of sail boats and more quirky furniture and a bathroom tiled in many bright colors. La Sebastiana sits at the top of a hill and rises up three stories, much more than the surrounding houses, like a castle. Its view of the city and the bay enviable of any other nearby. Such a view was fitting for a man who loved the sea and filled his house with small sailboats and nautical maps. I bought a copy of Neruda's memoirs and began to understand him more clearly through reading about his life in his own words. Much of these memoirs were written in the last couple years of his life right up until his death and were only published posthumously. When it came to politics, he often wrote bluntly throughout his memoirs of those people, actions and policies he disliked.

In his memoirs, Neruda made it clear that he was a passionate Stalinist. He even wrote poems, often cringeworthy, in praise of Uncle Joe. But after Stalin's death and the revelations by Khrushchev of the terrors committed during Stalin's reign, the whole of the left was thrown into turmoil. As appalled as most people were by Stalin's crimes and purges, Neruda took the news in stride, and still remained loyal to the cause of the USSR and belief that communist revolution was the best direction for equality in the wider world. Stalin's crimes were unquestionably embarrassing for those that blindly gave their support, and when the truth was known there was little to say and not really anyone to apologize to.

He dealt with the political fallout in a similar fashion of other Comrades. Like many Stalinists he had to deal with the political reality that came with the revelation of Stalin's crimes and was reluctant to apologize or change course – and could never say enough to repent for the sins of a man he supported so strongly. The left in the twentieth century was always splintering into different factions, and to further complicate Neruda's leftist credentials it is unsurprising that Neruda never publicly admitted that he deep down could not stand Fidel Castro, even after meeting him in Havana. As far as other events that notably led to splits among the left, a passionate denunciation from Neruda was similarly absent during the events in Prague in 1968. It was another event to split the left, and Neruda by then nearing the end of his life was set in his political beliefs, and some tanks in the street of a

Eastern European capital was somehow tolerable in order to see the communist ideology through. Political beliefs are never straightforward and with events changing as much as they did in Neruda's time there were many complex stances to be taken on an array of issues. Each further complicated by the next.

Through his memoirs I found that Neruda lived a decidedly restless life during his days of hiding in political exile out of necessity, but often of his own volition. That's why it appears odd for a man to have three houses. The houses in Santiago and Valparaíso were only built much later in life. By then he was a famous man of means and did as he pleased no matter how much it contradicted his politics. In fact he spent very little time at La Sebastiana, only towards the end of his life did he frequent all three. These three houses now sit elegantly as memorials to Neruda. It is not unusual for houses built by great men to often become a sort of mausoleum. It is a fitting paradox that Neruda needed three.

Neruda's complex character is best described by a man that knew him, Mario Vargas Llosa, the Peruvian Nobel Laureate and occasional politician met Neruda on several occasions as a young man. Vargas Llosa, who wrapped his career in politics with an unsuccessful run for President of Peru remembered meeting Neruda in Paris and described him in his collection essays, *Touchstones*, as "fat, friendly, gossipy, greedy." He specifically remembers the aging poet at a party commanding his wife, Matilde to, "'get over to that dish right now and save me the best bits.'"

Neruda always lived lavishly, and stories are rife of him indulging in lobster and fine wine, and generally living well even as a young man, before he gained fame as a poet. His treatment of his wives often closely resembling that to a butler or valet. During his time as a young diplomat in Sri Lanka and Burma he had servants who took care of nearly every domestic need including putting his towels on him after a bath and arranging his clothes. Vargas Llosa described in his collection essays, *Touchstones*, that, "One night, in Isla Negra, after an enormous meal, through half opened, tortoise eyes he looked at me and said that he had sent five signed copies of his latest book to five young Chilean poets. And not one of them wrote back to me," he complained sadly." Vargas Llosa further sheds light by saying, "There was something childlike about him, with his obsessions and desires that he expressed without any trace of hypocrisy, with the helpless enthusiasm of a naughty boy...this boy that he never stopped being.'"

It was only after reading Llosa's descriptions of Neruda that I understood the three houses and their contents and ultimately the man much more clearly. As is so often true of artists or cultural figures who take political stances, the man and the ideology are far from similar.

In his memoirs, Neruda writes effortlessly about his childhood, and the many phases of his life but always descends into politics with anger and derision in the way an old man predictably would. Any admirer of Neruda's poetry is eager to put the politics of Neruda aside. But to Chileans, Neruda the Poet and Neruda the Diplomat, the communist and politician, are one.

Of Neruda's three houses, Isla Negra was his favorite and the most sought out by admirers of his poetry and fellow admirers of his politics. It has been forever romanticized in his poems and he spoke lovingly about it in his memoirs. He even dreamed of it becoming a place where people would gather on the beach in front for talks and political gatherings. After seeing La Chascona and La Sebastiana it seemed silly not to make the short ride down the coast to get a glimpse of Isla Negra.

I took a bus from Valparaíso an hour south along the sandy coast and was dropped off at the main road a few hundred yards from the ocean. The bus driver pointed erratically in a few directions whilst continuing to look straight ahead, "Si, si, Isla Negra, Isla Negra." From where I stood, I could not see the ocean because of all the trees, and there was no sign posted for the house, but there were quite a few people making their way down a path through the trees. As I walked, the noise of a crowd and music grew rapidly, and I soon realized there were more than a few people curious to see Neruda's home by the sea. On a microphone, a woman rapidly espoused poetry before a small crowd circled around her. A couple yards down the path a band played rock music and when I could finally see the ocean, the path to it was lined with makeshift stalls of hippies selling homemade jewelry, clothing, and homemade snacks. The beach was dotted with large rocks, and littered with people, none of which were wearing a bathing suit nor interested in swimming. Some people lounged around on the rocks and others gathered around barbecues or under a canopied tent. Music blared from boom boxes. The red and blue flags flown on homemade flag poles whipped vigorously in the wind. The logo emblazoned on each of them was of a yellow hammer and sickle overlaid with an AK-47. A beautiful rocky beach looked an odd place for a political gathering no less one that took the shape of a Communist tailgate party. I made no mention of politics and did my best not stare at the couples napping on a towel wearing jeans and army boots. A fat communist is a peculiar description to reckon with but was fitting for the large mustachioed man who tended to the rack of ribs on the small grill in the sand.

Neruda's admirers were equally absurd in their exaggerated political beliefs. This was more like a half-assed cult than a political movement. They may as well have been a football team. The few I spoke to said they were from all parts of Chile and had always made an annual trek to Isla Negra. They cared little for Neruda's poetry and more for his Stalinism. This was a gathering of the Chilean Communist Party.

They were hanging out on the beach in front of Neruda's house just like he had wished they would. They were a rag tag group, a couple of fat guys paying far too much attention to the grill or laying on the beach in their jeans and boots. They were a sore sight spoiling the pretty coastline.

Walking up to the house I was surprised at how small it was. It was nothing grand, though the setting was fit for a grand mansion. The view out to the sea was as serene as any other and there seemed little reason to have a house anywhere else. There was a line of more than two hundred excited and pilgrim like people. I was discouraged by this, but forced myself to go in, because of how far I had come, and this was the last and most special of his three homes. It was a pleasure to walk around and see more of his trinkets and the view of the sea he had for so many years, in fact it was where he had spent much of the last few months of his life at the house working on his memoirs, while Chile slowly declined into political violence.

The house of a dead man is unquestionably a museum and a mausoleum. But the visitors at Isla Negra, were more like Pilgrims or worshippers. The people cried inside the house, holding their hands over their mouths to prevent themselves from being too loud. Some people I spoke to said they visited regularly or more than once. For Chileans, Isla Negra is a national monument and a memorial. A place, like Neruda himself that is imbedded in the conscience of Chileans. A place for him to be revered and obtain a kind of national immortality.

Neruda is not merely Chile's greatest poet, nor is he merely a man to be seen as a political symbol for the left, the working class and the disenfranchised, but he is a man who is inextricably tied to the conscience of Chile. I was all the more convinced of this at Isla Negra.

Neruda is not the country's only celebrated man to live in the collective conscience of the Chilean people. Right beside him is President Salvador Allende. These two men knew each other long before they were tied together in a collective and eternal martyrdom in the minds of Chileans and sympathetic foreigners.

Allende was born an aristocrat, but politically a Marxist, and naturally became a close friend of Fidel Castro. Though, Allende was a man who came from a family of means he thrived as a politician advocating for those without them. Before Allende was elected in 1971 Neruda was seriously urged to be the leader of the party but declined and gave way to the more seasoned career politician. Even though only a third of the country was Marxist, the government was indeed democratically elected. Thus Allende's democratic election was seen as a victory for those sympathetic to a Marxist ideology at home as well as abroad. The government led by Allende was quick to find support abroad in Fidel Castro who made a long tour across the country in 1972 giving speeches to students and workers alike and all those eager for support from Cuba and the USSR. Allende's policies of Nationalization were a perceived threat to the wealthy and even middle-class elements of the country as well as to the Nixon Administration who along with Secretary of State Henry Kissinger took it upon themselves to support an effort to have Allende overthrown. The subsequent coup was fast and effectively done through violent means. Allende being one of the earliest of the many casualties to come. He would commit suicide with a gunshot to his head on a couch in his office, before the military was able to reach him and likely do it themselves.

The leader of the coup came from within the ranks of the military as they so often do, led by a fellow party member and General Augusto Pinochet. Pinochet's almost thirty-year reign of terror, death and torture are a nightmare that Chileans continually attempt to exorcise. The horrors of the Pinochet regime are well documented in various forms.

****

During Allende's short reign as president, the aging Neruda was slowly dying from cancer and even with his Nobel Prize winning status had continued to be on the enemies list of the Right in Chile. Neruda lay sick in his bed when Isla Negra was raided in the lead up to the coup. But Neruda was not to suffer the same fate as his comrade Allende. For the young soldiers were too awestruck to do anything but apologize and leave swiftly without causing any more of a disturbance.

The legend of Neruda was already palpable before his death and had protected him from persecution. Neruda was spared for even the young soldiers sent to arrest him realized the sin they would be guilty of committing were they to kill the author of the Twenty Love Sonnets. His legend had spared him and in a sense his poetry had wielded power. He was more than just a political enemy on a list. Shortly thereafter would come Allende's death and a mere twelve days after Allende's death, the new military dictatorship quickly took hold of the entire country, and in a hospital in Santiago, Neruda succumbed to cancer.

Both deaths left the country traumatized and were the beginning of a traumatic period. Chile had found its human symbols that countries so often cannot do without. One a cultural and artistic icon, the other a democratically elected leader, both devoutly committed to a political ideology many had their hopes on for making a better nation.

Chilean politics had gone the same way as other South American nations for its short histories. From one coup to the next, each leader deposed without having left much of an impact of the nation let alone a lasting impression to unite around afterwards. The country had gone without a founding father type that a majority of Chileans could unite around. The leader of Chilean independence from Spain, Bernardo O'Higgins is a name one sees frequently on streets throughout Chile and he is a George Washington or Simon Bolivar type, but he is at the back of the minds of Chileans when it comes to what their nation is. With Allende and Neruda, Chile found its true symbols.

Allende and Neruda are continually praised and memorialized not just as a result of their perceived martyrdom, but because of the leadership and direction in which the country turned with the subsequent authoritarian regime led by Augusto Pinochet. Their deaths were considered an immediate lost of innocence, and all future hopes for a democratic nation were left to disintegrate in the hands of Pinochet. A nightmare like the Kennedy assassination, something that the country can never completely exorcise from its soul.

That is why Chileans will continue to flock to Isla Negra and keep remembering the leader of their country, Salvador Allende, who was the last hope before a long reign of terror, and they will always continue to find hope in the beautiful words of Pablo Neruda. Neruda on his own is much more interesting a man than his fellow martyr, chiefly for his powerful and prolific output of poetry.

Neruda indisputably died of cancer, but since the timing of his death nearly coincided with Allende's suicide and the overthrow of the country both are inevitably bound as one death in the minds of Chileans as too overwhelming to take as a natural occurrence or cruel coincidence.

People need martyrs and countries need founders - a kind of god or guiding light to look to. Chileans are most certainly justified in their hurt, not merely because of the events of Allende's disposal but because of what came to follow Allende and the brutality of Pinochet.

There is something a wider public does not like about artists getting too close to politics. Many people like their artists pure for some reason. It is a disgust that is simply explained by not wanting an artist to be spoiled by the awfulness of politics. Ideas have a way of spoiling art, because political statements are final, unlike the mystery and seduction of fiction, poetry and painting. Truth certainly exists in poetry, but it is always delivered with care. Politics is bluntness, especially for Neruda, personified.

It is a common practice to discount the political views of an artist, because it seems likely that they come from an uninformed place or the motivation is unknown. It is easier to handle the poet just being a poet rather than a poet/politician which comes across as much too complicated and unappealing. Neruda lived in an undoubtably political and tumultuous time, when it was nearly impossible to escape the political realities of the day, which were consequential to much of the world. In the world of Nazis and Communists, one often had to pick a side.

****

I had spent nearly two weeks in Valparaíso, enjoying the people and general happiness of the city. I found a used bookstore which I revisited a few times, that somehow had a large selection of mostly books in English. Getting lost in the writings of Neruda I was in a decidedly literary mood and ended up reading more than just Neruda. I had time to read a few short Gore Vidal novels, Robert Graves' *I, Claudius* - a short biography of Machiavelli and some stories by Turgenev and re-read Flaubert's masterful *Three Tales*.

I also bought a small copy of Flaubert's *Salammbo*, which turned out to be an unbelievably terrible book, and perhaps was not helped after reading *I, Claudius*.

My days were split into joyful literary expeditions followed by long walks through the city. Some days I would pick the most strenuous routes that were all incline, other days I took the funicular or a taxi to the top of the city and made my way back to the bottom always finding a more unique and colorful corner to investigate.

In the bars, restaurants and corner stores, wherever there seemed to be a television, it displayed the fighting which had flared up between Israel and Palestine the way it usually does every couple of years. While watching the ongoing clashes, taking in the reports of casualties, and hearing it all in Spanish in faraway Chile made the conflict seem all the more unsolvable and ultimately doomed. I did not pay too much attention, nor did the drinkers or diners of the restaurants and bars. They watched the footage of explosions and wounded being rushed into ambulances with attentive curiosity but went back to their drinks and conversations when the news had changed to something lighter. I did not give it much thought, but it was the main news story for a couple of weeks that had been escalating gradually to the stage of full on conflict that was unavoidable when looking at a television in a public place, opening up a newspaper or looking at any news source on the internet. I knew it was not entirely avoidable, but I did not expect to come across anything other than news about it whilst in Chile.

While walking back to my room one night I noticed a group of around seventy-five people gathering in a small urban park for a candle-lit vigil in solidarity with the Palestinians. Earlier in the day I saw a news report on a Chilean news channel talking about the deaths caused by Israeli bombing raids on Palestinian targets.

Young Chilean women wore revealing outfits but covered their heads with niqabs and hijabs. The irony seemed lost on them. The men wrapped red and white Keffiyehs around their necks. Some wore them draped over their shoulders. I stood by to watch and listen as they made short speeches denouncing Israel and praising Hamas' resistance to the Israeli forces.

I was reminded of all the things I had recently learned of Neruda's politics and his support for Stalin and all the contradictions that came along with it. The three houses, his lobster dinners and his devotion to material possessions and writing about love was mixed with an immovable devotion to authoritarian communist dictatorship. The paradox of his private life and his politics held a similar irony to those of the young women in revealing outfits who felt the need to cover their heads in solidarity with a distant cause. Some would arguably call it a solidarity of humanity despite a difference in culture, but it is undeniably absurd for western girls in a place as socially liberal as Chile dressed in such a way to show solidarity with a group so blatantly misogynistic among other prejudices as Hamas. But political belief and the desire to moralize in front of others so often trumps intellectual continuity and ideological consistency. Criticism of Neruda's politics has always been lessened by the beauty of his art. And perhaps the politics of these young girls were looked over as a result of their beauty or because no one cared to challenge a small gathering of protesters. They were not the poor working class of Valparaíso with beleaguered faces and calloused hands. They were resoundingly middle class, healthy, educated and notably white, holding signs in support of a group that is unalterably opposed to their own way of life.

Neruda's USSR was as far away as the young women's Gaza. Distant totalitarian cultures are inevitably seen through a lens not long enough to see that culture with an entirely clear view. Thus one forces its own desires and prejudices to form a narrative. Ultimately deciding that what they choose is inarguably correct, because they want something to believe in and a conclusion must be reached. A similar kind of politics festers in the United States and Europe, but it is nothing new. Perhaps that is the disadvantage of a place as isolated as Chile. Perhaps that is the difficulty distance brings to anyone seeking to understand any other place. Politics so often is simply blind faith. No less so in Chile. No less so than for someone as talented and eloquent as Pablo Neruda.

Poets are easy to love, especially after reading Neruda's poetry, he is, too. His faults as a person and his politics fall by the wayside. Nearly all the politics of individuals when placed under a microscope have evidence of the absurd, unreasonable and unrealistic. They are ultimately passions that are rarely expressed as beautifully as a poet would his verse. But a closer look at the man reveals an undoubtably complicated figure. Few poets, the great ones, are born with a soul of simplicity. I knew that Neruda was Chile's great man of letters, the continent's greatest poet, among the world's greatest ever, but most of all Neruda's life and words are the heart of a nation.

11

Easter Island

There is an island in the South Pacific where Spanish is spoken. In that language it is known as Isla de Pascua, in the language native to the Island it is known as Rapa Nui, but beyond the region it is widely known as Easter Island, named as such for being sighted on Easter Day by Dutch explorer Jacob Roggevenen. His sighting of the island was the first by European eyes and done so after a long arduous journey through the most barren part of the Pacific Ocean. Though, some still reach the island by way of large cruise ships, most people fly from Santiago. The six-hour flight is long in an age of speedy travel, but spotting the island from above after that many hours is no less exciting. Its remoteness makes the journey perceptively further. The pilots get a straight-ahead view during the long approach, but for the passenger the island appears suddenly with the circling of the plane towards the runway. The beauty of the island and its remote setting is striking and can leave one awestruck, flying for hours and only seeing clouds and water that appears perfectly still and peaceful from so high up. A yellowing-green suddenly appears in the enormous amount of blue along with the obvious shape of the Orongo crater from the air. It is so remote and lonely; the island looks as if it is lost and floating away.

There is a peculiar feeling that comes with looking down at the most remote place on earth and slowly descending towards it. I had thought that Patagonia was a place to disappear into, but this island looked even more of a place to vanish into and never be found again. The whole of its mass was surrounded by a white ring of relentless waves crashing upon its shores. Many islands have this necklace like feature and from such a high altitude it is a charming decoration, but the closer one gets it is easy to realize this ring is indicative of the massive and relentless power of the ocean surrounding the island.

Before I had ever left my own country, I often wondered what this distant island was like, what it was all about. From a distance it is endlessly peculiar and enticing. It was quirky on the surface and its remote location inevitably made it more of a mystery. This was the one place that always screamed of the exotic and unique, so different it was almost alien. It was a traveler's ultimate goal to get to this most distant of islands that was dotted with oversized statues which have been largely unexplainable as to how they were technically built and transported from one part of the island to another.

It was mostly undeveloped and like many islands the maintenance or rules of the road were obviously not much of a priority.

When I stepped into the dark reception area of the little hotel I found in Hanga Roa, I was met by a tall woman with a raspy but friendly voice. It is the kind of sound made by a person who is soon about to offer you some drugs.

I heard her American accent but for some reason did not think much of it. I figured the accent came from having learned English very thoroughly. When I gave back the little card she asked me to fill out with my home address and passport number her raspy voice repeated the name of the town I was from in the form of a question. I hesitated and said, "Yes."

"I'm from Larchmont."

It was stunning to go this far and meet an American from a town a few miles from my own living on the island. The remoteness of the island from home and most everywhere was quickly less of a barrier. Grace was from Larchmont, New York, and grew up around New York City. She worked at the Katonah Women's Prison, her aunt had a big art gallery in Chelsea, for all intents and purposes she was a New Yorker. After hearing all this it seemed almost unfathomable that she had firmly been settled on the island for over a decade. She had married a Rapa Nui man, had a child and slipped into island life, so she said. Each day Grace told me something about the character of the island, but on the first day, she said, sometimes things can get a little weird here. "Just be on the lookout for weirdness." Afterwards, the island seemed even more of a mystery and my curiosity only grew.

Before I had done much on the island, I let a few people back home know that I had gotten there safely and was planning out my next steps to begin exploring over the next few days. I was quickly made aware of something I was partially conscious of but had put at the back of my mind while dealing with the basic distractions that come with getting to a place so far away. When I sent messages home to my family that I had made it to Easter Island, I was surprised by the responses I had gotten in return. Over the past few weeks and months I had gotten a measured response when I said I had arrived in Punta Arenas or Santiago or in Buenos Aires, but when I got to Easter Island, they reminded me of something. They were joyous notes that collectively said, "Congratulations! You finally made it to Easter Island!" I had forgotten just how much I had spoken about wanting to go there when I was a teenager and into my twenties. More recently I spoke of it less and less, even though I continued to think about it. This somehow made the island a familiar sight, for I had poured over photos of the island and watched most every documentary there was about the island, and all of these visual memories were somehow made into real experiences. It was a real pleasure to be reminded of an old passion, and a long-held desire to be somewhere distant from home.

The excitement of my family for me was a satisfaction in itself, for someone had taken my desires into consideration all those years ago, and had remembered them, too.

That is why being reminded by my family of how much I had wanted to be on Easter Island was a pleasurable reminder of the past. It was as if I was skimming through my piles of books hoping to find one, I may have forgotten, only to be confronted with notes in the margins and carefully underlined sentences I had taken the time and care to remember. To encounter such a thing was to see myself, stilled in time. And with Easter Island those fine familial messages from thousands of miles away reminded me of the solitary thoughts of an earlier self, someone who had never really gone anywhere, and the distance I had recently traveled was all the more astounding to me. During my first night on the island I sat overlooking the sunset in Hanga Roa and thought of how I had dreamed of being in this place, and for most of the night I smiled for it felt like being in two places at once. Where was I? On an island or on an island in my dreams? Those messages allowed me to be in both.

I would make several journeys around the island, none more grueling than the next day when I set off onto the southern coastal road on a rented bicycle. Grace had warned me that it was not the easiest of rides and it involved quite a few hills sloping both up and downwards. She kept saying how hard it was, but I was so excited to see the rest of the island in the most down to earth ways. Getting a car seemed like a cop out, and I was determined to get as close to the island as I could. That meant working for it, seeing it slowly, and laboring across it unlike the van loads of tourists too old or tired to do the same. It was too far to walk to the other side of the island, and the eleven miles across looked possible on a bike. I had not ridden a bike in many years and my excitement blinded me from how unprepared I was for the road I was about to traverse.

It was a deceivingly easy ride at first, and once I reached the outskirts of Hanga Roa, I was swiftly riding down a large hill, so fast at times, that I slowed myself so as not to fall, and was greeted with a beautiful view clear across the barren landscape and out to the immense ocean beside it. Whatever closeness to home I had felt as a result of meeting Grace, subsided with the sight of just how large and invincible the ocean was before me. It made the island and everything on it look vulnerable and about to be washed away at any moment. The sky never ceased to change with the weather, and as I rode across the patchy road I was met with wind so strong it would turn a flat section of road into a steep incline and when it came from the side I often lost my balance, having to walk until it subsided or blew in a more favorable direction. I was forced to stop to rest and took the opportunity to watch the incessant ocean crash into the rocks. The water looked like a wild animal just as it had on the eastern shores of Patagonia.

Cars, vans and minibuses would suddenly appear on the narrow road over hilltops and nearly collided with me on a few occasions. It was a barren landscape with dangers and difficulties at most every turn. The murky sky made me aware of the potential for a terrible storm, fit with monsoon-like rain, lightning strikes and even hail. The wind blew in ways that directly affected my riding of the bike that it was as if someone was controlling it from a switch board. It was an unforgiving set of circumstances and made me more aware why most people simply got in a car to get across to the sights at the other side of the island. The way the bike hurt me made me feel like an old man. It was embarrassing to even think of terms like saddle sores. Halfway through the journey it was so painful to sit on the rickety bike that I stood and peddled as much as possible, only adding to the difficulty of the ride. I knew I would see more of the island and see it more thoroughly, and only stubbornness and determination would make that so. Eleven miles was too far to walk and not really practical without a plan as how to get back other than walking another eleven miles. I had a week to see the rest of the island, so I was in no rush. I could rent a car another day.

Halfway across the island I reached a single large Moai called Te Ara O Te Moai, surrounded by a little fence, fallen over on its face and visibly eroded from the fierce wind the south side of the island is constantly faced with. It was dumbfounding to see an archaeological treasure lying on the ground at this distant spot next to the ocean. I soon realized Easter Island was a museum to itself, many of the statues remained where they had always stood, some raised up once again, while others were left fallen over in a symbolic and almost decadent fashion. This single Moai was in a most dramatic setting that would make any sculptor enviable to have their work set amongst. Though Easter island had always been a primitive place distant from all the modern creations of man, it was still littered with the decadent doings and results of human nature. Its barren and almost ruined state is the result of man's instincts to cultivate power by creating gods to worship, cults to join and symbols such as the Moai, to worship. This was the first of many large Moai I would see fallen over, indicative of the fate of the society from which they had sprung, and a reminder of the fragility of anything made by man.

At times, it was frightening to think of how remote I was, but as I went up each hill I could see more clearly across the island and it became an almost private place of my own. There was certainly no one else on a bike and every car or minibus quickly disappeared.

There was one lonely coconut tree on a hill that could be seen for a couple miles. Grace referred to it as Coco and also said that it kind of teases you as it appears closer than it is but then you turn round a bend and have to snake your way around more road, up and down until finally reaching it. From there, it was a couple more miles to the entrance of Rano Raraku and the incline steadily grew.

When I was just about there, I saw a pickup truck stopped in front of the quarry and the Moai that dot its southern face. On the gravelly road adjacent to the quarry two girls stood on the bed of a pickup truck taking pictures. I was struggling with the incline made more difficult by the loose gravel. I noticed them catch their first glimpse of me and the expressions on their faces were a mix of confusion and amazement. One double-looking at me as I got closer, the other just stared and I quickly realized what a crazy endeavor it was to ride the rickety bike all that way.

The one girl continued to stare before saying, 'Where are you going?' Which felt a rather strange question considering I was heading down a dead-end road to a tourist attraction in the form of a giant quarry directly in front of us. She was shocked to see someone riding a bike and we both laughed at her question. They offered me a ride and suddenly I was a hitchhiker for the last few hundred yards to the small welcome center. I had ridden the bike a strenuous eleven miles only to be driven the last few hundred yards.

Martine and Lucia were from Toronto, but hurriedly explained they were of Polish extraction, their parents being refugees who fled USSR controlled Poland in the eighties. Both were quick witted and funny as Canadians tend to be, each with a sense of humor that could belong to someone who is professionally funny. I knew they had taken pity on me for the tired state I must have looked but they also asked me to join them for another reason. They complained about some 'gorilla-like' Polish men whom they were sat next to on the plane from Santiago and who had failingly tried to woo them. They happened to be at the quarry as we arrived and the girls only talked of them in the most insulting ways, calling them baboons, idiots, blockheads and a litany of other animal related insults. Nearly everyone was a tourist but the two men, looked even more so, and they were a visible eyesore even from across the parking lot. Luckily, we never had to speak to them.

We toured around Rano Raraku and then up to the crater lake and back down to Ahu Tongariki, speaking in questions about everything we saw, doing our best to play anthropologists on the go. I was so tired from the bike ride and now concerned with being politely social to the girls that I could barely process the beauty of the statues dotted around the face of the quarry. I went at the pace the girls went, and did what they wanted to do, because I knew there was no way I could ride the few miles to the road that went through the center of the island and another eleven miles back to Hanga Roa. I was more than relieved to be riding around in a truck and not on the bike anymore. The longer I sat in the car the more I realized how crazy it was to ride a bike across the island, and how much longer it would have taken to get back to Hanga Roa.

We stopped along the way to sit and gaze out at the ocean on Anakena beach where the weather had become sunny and the gloomy skies on the south side of the island had shifted out over the ocean and were soon nowhere to be found.

We hung out in the sand all fully clothed and drifting off into deep relaxation. I was exhausted from the bike ride, the climb up the quarry and relieved to be laying down. I was also grateful for these two girls insisting on giving me a ride without ever asking for it. Even here the kindness of strangers could be found.

They dropped me off just before Hanga Roa and I rode back while they went north to see some more of the Moai. I woke up from a nap just in time to meet them for dinner. They brought some other people they had just met at the little hotel where they were staying. We had a big table in a small restaurant overlooking the sea and together we quickly got drunk and afterwards filled the little windswept streets with raucous laughter. The streets were deserted, and no locals hung about.

They dropped me back off at my little hotel that I could barely see for the lack of streetlights or any other kind of lights near the hotel. I was exhausted, but I had made it to the other side of the island and back and made friends along the way.

I was drunk and unsuccessfully fighting off the mosquitoes that had snuck into my room, but as I slowly succumbed to the alcohol and soreness of my body, I lay in bed satisfied in having chosen to go across that southern road in such an arduous manner so that each of its hills could remain with me and I with it.

****

The next day, Grace was waiting for me in the bamboo lobby to ask me how sore my body was. She had seen countless people try the same thing and end up barely able to walk the next day. That was the state my body was in. But I had no intention of hanging around and Grace told me where I could rent a car. Less than a half hour after picking it up for which they offered no insurance and seemed as though it was about to fall apart at any moment I was back out in the middle of the south road gazing at the Te Ara O Te Moai again and another sinister sky that came with the morning shift in weather. I stopped at several secluded spots to gaze out to the ocean before navigating a few rock ledges down to the water to gaze across the shoreline, each time getting a more complete view of the island. I looked and looked down each side of the coast and to the cloudy horizon but there was no rain, just crashing waves and lots of wind pelting some little rock islands a few hundred yards off the coast. I wondered how long it would be before the entire island would break off like that and crumble into the sea. My body was sore and the few hundred feet I walked from the rickety car were painful, but I was much more able to drink in the island and not have to worry about traversing all the hills I would encounter again.

I returned to Rano Raraku and slowly walked around the Moai, finding that I was often the only one there. I took a closer look at the same statues I had seen the day before, enjoying their quirky shapes and the beauty of the setting. Where the Moai are finished and standing they give something to the spot where there was once nothing and that is enough, the faces, expressions and styles (standing, kneeling, sitting) added a little something each time. At varying speeds, they become something — symbols, temples, idols and even Gods. There was a pleasant view of Ahu Tongariki in the distance that was an obvious place of ritual, the statues are natural symbols of idolatry. Within Islam, the reasoning for the banning of the creation of symbols of idolatry becomes obvious on Easter Island, for symbols such as the Moai naturally have an intoxicating affect upon those confronted with them.

One statue nearly finished but still not cut out from the mountain, so large it was almost too big to move and thus abandoned. It made the carving process much more vivid and the harshness of the work could be more easily imagined. For a brief moment I walked in the shoes of those faced with the job of getting these stones out of the mountain.

I eagerly walked around to the crater behind the quarry to explore and this time walked around to the top of the low side of the crater, the inland side, to sit and gaze at the whole of the crater's lake and up towards the top of the quarry. Its non-existent peak chipped away into a sinking u-shape obviously done by man. Behind me was the whole of the island, the sun shining brightly upon the dry and yellowed grass of winter. The wind was fierce in this spot, but it was yet another isolated and peaceful place to rest. The longer I sat the more I enjoyed the view of the quirky site before me. When the few visitors disappeared from the main entrance in the distance, I thought I was alone, and this spot had become my own personal possession.

I looked to my left and was met with the sight of a large pack of wild horses who had swiftly climbed the other side of the crater and paused momentarily at the top before charging down towards the lake to drink. The horses were a peaceful and majestic sight. Though, they are no secret it felt a stroke of luck to see them in one of the island's most unique spots. Luck happens in such places and it was an exhilarating experience to watch them run. I continued around the top edge of the crater and slowly walked up towards the top of the quarry which faces the ocean. Anywhere else this seemed like a place that would be off-limits to a tourist or traveler or anyone without 'authorization,' but there were no such rules here. The top of the crater was wide enough so there was little risk of falling off the backside of the quarry whilst navigating the thorny bush dotted path. While I sat at the top and looked back at the island the horses had finished with cooling off by the lake and ran up the crater once more and disappeared down the other side. It was exhilarating to watch them run in a pack. The sun was beating down and the wind whipped across even harder.

The quarry itself was a kind of open-air temple, something to love and come to in the same way one would an empty church. I thought of how these statues were created as a form of worship and idolatry and from that it created a new kind of life for the island. A life which was ultimately based in utilizing its limited resources that naturally led to the downfall of the island's life and society. This quarry was the island's Parthenon, and such is the uniqueness of this place that you can sit atop it's ruined temple. There was the beautiful sight of the ocean with sun all over it and suddenly I realized its true height when I got to the edge. From the top of the quarry, there is an overwhelming and broad view of the ocean which makes the island and the quarry itself incredibly small and weird. From this height Ahu Tongariki and its row of fifteen Moai now looked a miniature ant like version of what I had seen up close the day before. It was a place littered with the remnants of the efforts of human beings.

As I drove around the island re-visiting the sights of the day before I came across the horses in a few more places, and at times they followed me and walked up to me when I was stopped on the north side of the island to observe some fallen Moai. I went around the island watching, following, being followed by the herd of horses who had run up and out of the crater lake. Many of them were young and jumped and bucked often. I sat at some of the Moai on the north side of the island and the horses walked right up to me. There was something surreal about wild horses running beside the ocean.

Again, I hung out at Anakena Beach and watched a dark rain cloud heading towards the island. Then back to Hanga Roa across the island, I more clearly realized there were views of the whole island from its middle, the ocean could almost always be seen. The barrenness of the island puts one in the mindset that all the animals have gone with the destruction of trees, the lack of sound from birds is deafening but easily gotten used to and the sight of any animal is an exciting event.

The next day I returned to the southern coastal road again and stopped at many of the secluded spots. I decided not to visit the quarry again, but naturally saw it from most every spot I was whilst being on the southern coast. I preferred to look at it from a distance. The little coastal road was firmly implanted in my mind, all the colors, all the wind and sun and water I could easily feel just thinking about it.

****

I caught a ride up to the top of the Orongo crater which was surrounded completely by the clearest blue skies. I was sensitive to them as most every day I had been on the island there was some kind of rain shower or lingering of dark clouds. This was a pleasant surprise that gave the natural beauty of the island and the Pacific a more cheerful background. The little village at the crater's edge, with its low stone walled huts blended nicely into the setting and had a perfect view of the 'bird man' rocks that sit majestically a few hundred yards offshore. It felt a decidedly different place to the rest of the island. Being at the top of the cliff makes it possible to only see the crater and the ocean beside it, the rest of the island is naturally hidden away. The sun is direct and heavy but the wind not as bad.

There was a guide giving a lecture to a group on the life of locals over hundreds of years and how the huts were a place of refuge for some of the island's rulers over the centuries. It sounded similar to that of many other cultures, and I did my best to listen, but was more interested in the natural beauty of the setting. A colorful array of flowers grew along the inside walls of the crater, its shape was otherworldly and would have been just as applicable for it to be on some part of the moon. The backside of the crater had been slowly eroding for countless years and looks like a metaphor for the rest of the island. The elements had chipped away at its surface just as the inhabitants of the island chipped away at the peak of the Rano Raraku quarry. I no longer thought of the unnatural gap in the quarry's peak as something entirely exploited as the elements were acting similarly to the inhabitants of the island with a nearly indistinguishable result. It is a matter of time before the wall collapses and the crater becomes a cove for the ocean to nestle into, getting a chance to slowly erode the crater's inner walls.

In Patagonia, I was not surprised to watch large chunks of ice at the Perito Moreno Glacier break off into the water below, for it was ice and however much or little temperatures are changing it was bound to come crashing down at some point as all the ice of the glacier reaches its endpoint after coming down from the mountains of southern

Patagonia. However, the Orongo crater and the rest of the island was made of earth. It was not as delicate as ice and vulnerable to a simple change in temperature. This was earth, rock, land, whatever you may call it, being taken apart by wind and water. It leaves one in despair to see it slowly fall. There is no rebuilding an island such as this. It is a precious jewel and no matter how tough and resilient its rocks may be, they will fall just as its society had done centuries ago.

As beautiful as the crater, the ocean view and the bird-man rocks were that day, I walked down the back of the crater towards Hanga Roa in a decidedly despondent mood over the eventual fate of the island. I was sad to think that this mysterious and magical place would somehow cease to be. I felt lucky in knowing that I lived to see it, for I lived in the time when it was still far enough from its eventual fate. Easter Island, like many other islands has a natural beauty. A beauty that is bound in its vulnerability to the more powerful elements of the earth. A beauty that exists and is heightened because it will soon disappear.

Islands are a symbol of the end and islands are the elderly of the earth. Land dies slower than everything but perhaps their slow death is what makes them so graceful and beautiful and so sadly missed before they have even gone. I never knew that a piece of land could fill you with such heartfelt feelings. That is because when something is so close to its end, it is natural to see it as already gone.

I found myself walking in the street and a man in the distance was walking towards me. He was disheveled and easily recognizable as something other than a local. No Rapa Nui, no matter how poor they were, looked as frazzled and carelessly dressed as this man who was crossing to my side of the street to talk to me. I guessed he was an American before he revealed he was Roy from both Phoenix, Arizona and Rochester, New York. With long hair like a modern-day hippie and teeth sufficiently British of any era, he only talked of drugs – mostly of doing Ayahuasca in Iquitos, Peru for three weeks. He kept saying how it was better than any other drug. He told me how he saw me from the bus the other day while I took the long walk down from the crater. He could not believe how crazy it was that I decided to walk that far on the steep hill. While he said I was crazy, I thought of all the Ayahuasca he had taken. It was another thing that seemed to make me stand out just as riding the bike had to the Canadian girls.

He said he planned on getting in the weed business when he got back home, but things were not up and running at the moment, because they were in the development stages. Colorado was way too structured already and corporate, he argued. Northern California or Oregon were his targeted markets. He said that weed and Ayahuasca saved his life, because he used to be three hundred pounds and had PTSD from serving in the Iraq War. He talked about drugs like a missionary preaching Christ and I could not help but believe him for he seemed content and eager to make others feel as he felt and see what he saw. Later that night as I sat in the small harbor of Hanga Roa looking at the purple sunset I thought of what those leaves from the Amazon did for him and I felt the same about what the rocks of Easter Island had done for me.

12

Iquique - Arica - Tacna

When I returned from Easter Island I was back in Santiago without much of a plan other than to head north by bus, but I had not given it much thought, it was very late, and naïvely I assumed I could easily get a bus all the way to Iquique. It was nearly eleven o'clock at night when it turned out I had just missed the last bus heading north. I sat in the large bus station watching it slowly empty out thinking that six hours was not a long time to wait for the earliest bus to leave the next day. After I had just sat on the plane for six hours that amount of time seemed like it would move quickly. An hour later all that was left were a few janitors and security guards and when they saw me sitting there reading a book, they told me I had to go as overnighting was not allowed. When I walked outside, I was met with a temperature that had steadily fallen in a couple hours into the thirties and I was unprepared for that kind of cold. I was discombobulated having gone from a tropical island setting in the middle of the Pacific Ocean to the far end of a cold dark city in a matter of hours. I felt grateful to still have my large winter coat with me that I had seen as a burden when being in places like Easter Island and Valparaíso, but now it was entirely necessary. I knew I would've been in trouble had I not had it.

I went to the closest hotel and they said they had no rooms and I was not allowed to hang around in the lobby either. The next closest hotel was full and the same rules applied with regards to their lobby. There were no cabs in sight and none of the local buses stopped anywhere near the bus station. The buses were lit up brightly inside with a few tired passengers zooming by to the comfort of their beds. It was now two thirty in the morning and the more I looked for a place to sleep I could not find one. It was odd to be in this predicament, that is, being stranded. I was not exactly in the middle of nowhere, I was in a city and a very big one at that, but every option of getting anywhere seemed to quickly be taken away. A part of me felt like I was supposed to be scared and some of the streets I went down were eerily empty and disheveled but for some reason they did not look menacing. I saw a man sleeping peacefully on the street with his head leaned up against a wall and his hands tucked into his pockets – even the homeless looked peaceful and safe out in the streets of Santiago. I circled back towards the bus station seeing if I could get back in as it was now three o'clock in the morning and I was not only getting colder but slowly becoming more tired, too. The janitors outside showed no pity, but walked one block over with me and pointed down a long shady alley and said "barrio, barrio," which was in the direction of some awful boarding houses. I walked halfway down that street before deciding to turn back and take my chances elsewhere. There were still no taxis and all the buses were now completely gone and walking towards the center of the city would take at least an hour in what was now a temperature close to freezing. My phone was dead and at this hour the two reasonable looking hotels had locks on their doors. There was one miniature motel that had all its lights on, but the doors were locked, and nobody was at the desk. I walked another mile or so and found a decrepit looking place that had a clean hallway which gave me a glimmer of hope. I pressed against the buzzer and waited a few minutes thinking nothing would happen, but then one of the most beautiful women I have ever seen came down the steps and through the long hallway to open the door for me. She had the calm demeanor of someone who had spent her entire life in this rundown neighborhood near the Santiago bus station. She looked at me like she had seen more than a few lost and clueless foreigners in her life. I felt decidedly lucky and entirely grateful to this girl. She gave me my key and I went up to the little shabby room that had constant noise from passing buses and cars and was only slightly warmer than the temperature outside. But my fingers were no longer freezing nor was the rest of my body. It was only earlier that day that I was literally drinking out of a coconut and sitting on a beach. I only managed to sleep for an hour or so because of the noise but I still felt happy to be able to rest in a bed surrounded by four walls, and a locked door.

After a few hours I had to get back to the bus station for the long ride north and in my tired state I settled my bill of twenty dollars. I stepped onto the street before walking back to the bus station to get on the bus to the north of Chile. In my sleepless state, I again underestimated how long the ride was.

****

Twenty-four hours later the bus arrived in Iquique and it was no longer cold or dark. The ride was so long we had crossed into another climate and even though I was staring at the Pacific Ocean I was at the edge of the world's largest desert, the Atacama. Now standing in an increasingly hot and dry city I felt I had nearly traversed the full spectrum of climates in forty-eight hours. From tropical island to a cold city and now a desert. I had thought little of the changing climates I had been traversing over the last couple of months, but it made the geography of the continent all the more vivid. The diversity of climates and the sheer size of the continent struck me as awesome and I now felt the distances I had traveled in a more tangible way. So much of getting across such distances required endurance of a mental rather than physical sort. The physical part was easy and taken care of by noisy buses and trains. The distance and the time it forces upon you requires a kind of cerebral patience from those who seek to test it.

It was winter in the southern hemisphere and that seemed an inarguable fact in places like Punta Arenas and Santiago but while my arm shaded my eyes from the sun, sand blew across the streets and I watched bikini clad girls walk towards the ocean carrying surf boards I was forced to expand my definition of winter.

It was also at this point that I realized how addicting traversing great distances can be and I was somewhat stricken with this addiction. I had done long overland journeys before, both in Asia, one from Shanghai to Bukhara, and another from Beijing to St Petersburg. But at this point, this journey started to feel different than the others. This one was longer in time and through more countries. I had spent almost a week combined sleeping full nights on buses and sometimes an entire day. All three journeys were similar in distance and difficulty but the diversity of landscape of the South American continent never ceased to be an astounding revelation. When one goes from Siberia to Moscow it is impossible to forget you are looking out at Russia the whole way and the same can be said for much of China outside of its cities. South America's diversity of landscape makes it a world unto itself and traversing its mass was like circumnavigating a planet and to traverse the earth now seemed like space travel. The abundance of geographical change often confused me as to knowing what country I was in. My ignorance to the natural character of each country was just as astounding and each arrival was a kind of epiphany.

I thought of it as a kind of addiction because even though arriving in Iquique was satisfying, I could not wait to cross into Peru. Even though I had just gotten off a twenty-four-hour bus ride it was an action I could not get enough of. To myself, I frequently compared traveling to mountain climbing for the obvious aspirational connotations that climbing mountains invokes. The few small mountains I had climbed were certainly a challenge, but I never felt fulfilled in climbing upwards in the same way I do from traversing distances whether it be walking or some kind of transport. After getting off the bus in Iquique, mountain climbing seemed a hollow endeavor, a somewhat artificial journey, for one was always faced with the immediate disappointment of having to turn around and climb down the mountain to where you started. I preferred traveling across rather than up for there is nearly no end to traveling across. For the mountain climber there is a determined end to each journey but for the walker, the wanderer, and the nomad the journey ends when you say so. It ends when you get too tired and feel like sitting for a while in one place. With climbing, the arrival never sufficiently satisfied me, and the prize was more in seeing the view or the untouched landscapes that exist at the tops of mountains.

After all the hours on the bus, I also enjoyed being physically exhausted but exhilarated by how I was still mentally energized and ready to go anywhere, at this point that still meant going North. Perhaps this was a harmless addiction, noble to a degree, but inarguably satisfying and I philosophically thought for a moment that the untraveled life is not worth living. Even while I pondered this thought, I knew that Borges still occupied a small space in my bag and I was reminded of my enjoyment of other states of being. I smiled contentedly, not wishing to confine myself to a philosophy of any sort and was somewhat assured in the belief that there was room for both.

Iquique was a sleepy place that had pockets of liveliness and a market with food stalls of short Peruvian ladies selling homemade food that was utterly delicious. Their presence made it evident that Peru was nearby, more so than the rest of Chile. The ocean was a complimentary sight to the heat that became more oppressive by mid-afternoon.

All roads lead to the fish markets next to the harbor that sold small plastic containers of various kinds of ceviche for a few pesos. The harbor was overcrowded with fishing boats docked in seemingly random places.

The men perched at each stall shouted for attention and organized the deli containers that were packed with the colorful varieties of ceviche. Each container was an exotic mix of colors and flavors. Everything had the taste of citrus and not only did it leave traces of citrus in your mouth but made you feel as though your whole pallet had been washed and cleansed. I bought three different kinds but there were locals that left with stacks of them in plastic bags. There was no other kind of food in sight or nearby, everyone was mad for ceviche. The little mixtures were a refreshing anecdote to the dry heat.

Large seals swam and crowded around the docks as fishermen and passers-by threw fish out to them and we all reveled in the scrum of seals that ensued in the water. Few parts of the harbor were left without the doglike face of a seal poking its whiskers out of the oily water. There was hardly a lamp post or edge of a building without a long row of imposing pelicans angling their long beaks towards the street and the harbor. Each pelican inspected everything like it was food, even the people. While perched high up they were a stoic and authoritative sight, but when they sprung out to fight over some fish they were without grace and became nasty to anything nearby. Gradually the seals crept up on to some small patches of sand beside the harbor to rest and be fed by fishermen and I suppose get away from unreasonable seals. They found comical challenges from small dogs let off their leash. The seals remained none to fussed by the neurotic barking of beagles and terriers. Some seals made their way into the sunny spots of the parking lot to bathe on the warmed up asphalt, but could find no peace on the land for here they were met by the opposition of a pair of winos eager to give a piece of their mind about who this sunny patch of parking lot belonged to.

It was a relief to not have to search for a room in the cold of Santiago and Iquique was simply a pleasant place to take in and to be. I had easily found a place to stay but it was a city that seemed pleasant enough to sleep outside. I found much more peace than the seals and took advantage of the warm sun that divided its light between the ocean and the edge of the desert. I walked along the water to the other more residential side of the city where the seals had also migrated to the dock of another fish market where the fishermen took great pleasure in feeding the seals. This pack of seals was much larger and more rambunctious, barking deeply at one another and recklessly jumping off rocks on top of each other for the buckets of fish hurled into the ocean. Seagulls and pelicans did their best to pick off what they could and dogs gathered at the edges of the dock to neurotically bark at the seals. It was a peculiar sight to see two mammals bark at each other, one from the land the other from the ocean.

It was a great excitement to watch such large creatures beside the simple dock. Elsewhere, it was a show that people would travel great distances and buy tickets to see. But a couple dozen one thousand-pound seals hurling themselves on top of each other was more or less a regular occurrence in Iquique. Some cities have pigeons, but Iquique has seals and after a couple hours of hanging by the docks they became as normal a presence as pigeons in Central Park.

The heat could only be mitigated by two things, taking a swim at one of the narrow beaches alongside the coastal road where young kids made failed attempts to surf the small waves or escape inside for a siesta. I did a little of both and by the time darkness had fallen a small stage had been set up alongside the market in the main square.

It was mostly rap and dance music. At one point they even played Kriss Kross' 'Jump' while three people did their best to mimic American street double-Dutch. A song I had not heard for more than ten years. The crowd enjoyed the show and it was congenial enough, but I enjoyed it for other reasons.

Music is something that is mostly done well and to the highest level in the United States and also in Britain and Australia. Music in the rest of the world usually takes on a more ceremonial or cultural character that lacks most any kind of individuality. There are few places where music breaks from longstanding traditions in the way that music in the United States does. Music outside of America or Britain is almost always a comical sight, especially whenever there is an attempt to mimic American music, more specifically rap and hip-hop. Most any attempt at rap music by anyone who is not African American quickly takes the shape of a comedy show whether the performer knows it or not. And the further it gets from the Bronx, Compton or Chicago the more absurd and laughable it becomes. It is not solely a matter of race for it even lacks authenticity and is rarely convincing in African countries. I once watched a hip-hop show in a Tokyo nightclub and as serious as they were about the performance it was difficult to not see the humor in it. But impersonation really is a kind of flattery and for hip-hop to be the preferred musical entertainment in a city beside the Atacama Desert and not something of a more local character speaks to how unique and popular hip-hop music is. It was a fun reminder of home and as distant as Iquique was from New York or Los Angeles or even from Santiago, it momentarily felt close to home.

As pleasant as Iquique was it was difficult not to see it as a refuge beside a harsh desert that was the largest in the world. It was possible to walk from one end of the city to the other in an afternoon and driving to each end took minutes. It was a speck compared to the immensity of the Atacama. Though the desert always appeared a dangerous and uninhabitable place it was not bereft of people. In fact it was a place that has more than a little life to it. Beneath its harsh surface is an ocean of lucrative mineral mines for which corporations and countries have often struggled for control. It is often argued that these mines played a large part in the decision to overthrow Allende in 1973. Allende had begun a series of nationalizations of certain sectors of the economy which evoked corporations along with Nixon and Kissinger to worry it was only a matter of time before Allende would seize control of the mines of the Atacama.

Directly east of Iquique was the mining town that grew famous for thirty three men being trapped when a mine collapsed and the long rescue operation that ensued amidst a growing personal drama around some of the miners who found concern not only from wives and family members but from mistresses, too. A movie, books and even appearances on American talk shows and a few minutes of fame were the result.

There were a few abandoned mining towns that took on the inevitable description of ghost towns. They were a few hours into the desert and finding a ride out that way proved all too fruitless. Working mines were privately owned for the most part and were not in the business of giving tours of their dangerous extraction activities to nosey foreigners not looking to invest, so I decided to push on towards Arica.

****

The closer I got to Peru the more eager I became to cross the border. I had been in Chile for nearly a month and the border with Peru was looking more like a finish line even though I was to continue north to Puno, Cusco, and on to Lima.

The road to Arica diverged inland before curving back out towards the coast and this inner landscape, which I realized was not even at a quarter of the desert's width, was even drier and more desperate. The heat more oppressive and any view worth stopping to gaze at became a hurried affair for there was nowhere from which to escape these unfriendly elements.

Arica was a frontier town and the presence of a nearby country and its border and the people of various nationalities along with Chileans and Peruvians coming and going made it all the more a jovial crossroads. The border with Peru was only a few miles away, but this was still resoundingly Chile.

Made evidently so by the presence of an enormous flag on the top of the Morro de Arica, a large boulder shaped hill near the city's coastline. The Morro de Arica was successfully captured by Chilean forces during the War of the Pacific and today looks out over the ocean, the city's harbor that is shaped like a crooked finger and on a clear day one can see across the border into Peru.

The tensions that had been steadily rising during the first three quarters of the 19th century would lead to the War of the Pacific which took place between 1879 and 1883. Though, there were a number of small reasons for the conflict between Chile and Bolivia who formed an alliance with Peru, the war was ultimately made possible over a dispute concerning borders. The lands within these territories were not just valuable for their access to the Pacific but mainly for the valuable mineral deposits beneath them.

Chilean mining interests had come under increased taxation from the Bolivian government which prompted the Chileans to occupy areas in and around their mining operations and then some. Tensions quickly rose and it was not long before Bolivia declared war on Chile, ultimately supported by Peru. The war was particularly nasty between the three parties with battles taking place in some of the harshest areas of the Atacama Desert.

The war was only brought to a close after four years when the Chileans enlisted the help of the British in a series of well-planned assaults by both land and sea. The British backed assaults were too great for the insufficiently equipped and less organized Peruvian and Bolivian forces. Chile signed a peace deal with Peru and a number of concessions were made in both directions but ultimately the Chileans came out on top with more territory and had to send money the other way in the form of war reparations. Bolivia lost the most territory in the fight, ultimately signing a truce with Chile and for several decades afterwards would be forced to sign a few more treaties which handed over even more land. This resulted in Bolivia losing its Pacific coastline forever making it a landlocked country. The city of Arica had once been a part of Bolivia, but now it undeniably belonged to Chile.

Having gone through a good portion of the Chilean part of the desert I got a sense of just how brutal a landscape in which each side had fought and later when I crossed into Peru, this sense of brutality only grew, for so did the harshness of the desert.

I was fascinated by this war not only because of the extreme conditions in which the war was fought or that it led to a great shifting of the borders of three nations, but also because it is a largely unknown war outside of the countries that fought in it. To much of the rest of the world this is an insignificant conflict and most certainly obscure. A conflict in which twenty thousand people died and a further twelve thousand were wounded. The Atacama was not just an unforgiving place of heat and isolation, it was a battlefield. A place where a real war had been fought for each of its unforgiving miles of sand and rock. Even this place was something people were willing to fight and die for.

We are inundated with story after story of World War II and the Vietnam War and we regularly seek to exorcise the ghosts and consequences of the Civil War, but the War of the Pacific made me look at lists of other wars that have been fought in South America and I came to find that there were dozens, nearly hundreds of them of various scales. The wars that settled the borders of South American countries and pushed them back and forth over the centuries have gone almost completely unnoticed by the rest of the world. It was natural to conclude that there are always wars, but not all of them will be remembered.

There was no sign of hostility in Arica past or present for the city was just as congenial as Iquique for its frontier character and the peculiar sight of surfers with stereotypically long blonde hair from America and Australia, giving it a party atmosphere. The border gave the sense of excitement and anticipation in both directions. Much of Chile was unknown to those who had just crossed the border and Peru was unknown to those that waited patiently in Arica. Many of those hanging around the city's bars and restaurants were here to surf the exceptional waves that break just north of the city before the border.

At night, the city's main pedestrian street took on a jovial atmosphere with each restaurant, cafe, and bar filled with drinkers and people watchers. Many tables were filled with the young blonde men chatting about this thing or that. Policemen with large revolvers calmly patrolled the streets while people bustled around them with a thrilling energy fueled by the intoxicating air of a city next to the ocean. It seemed as though the night would never end, and no one wanted it to end.

I had gone the length of Chile and had never seen another country, perhaps besides the United States change so many times in its geographical character. Punta Arenas now seemed a world away in time and distance and where I had started in São Pãolo was even further. I now felt myself feeling sad to leave Chile, but I was ready to move forward and into Peru.

It was an odd process getting across the border to Peru. I went to the large parking lot filled with taxis waiting to fill up their cars, usually with six people. We got in the car and waited. When there were enough people the driver took all our passports and walked across the parking lot to have something done to them. I sat there for a few minutes wondering if this was some sort of scam. The people in the back holding their baby looked nonplussed about it, but I had no clue where this man went and I was at the furthest end of a country that had taken me more than twenty-five hours to get to overland, and without my passport I would not even be able to get on a bus back to Santiago. I had gone the length of Chile and was now only interested in getting across the border to Peru. So to make sure the driver was doing what he was supposed to I took the keys out of the car and went looking for him. I went over to the long building that had door after door of travel agent type set ups and could not find him. On the other side of the building was the same set up and it was only at the last one that I found him with all our passports being looked over and stuffed with pieces of paper to get us through Chilean customs. Relieved that he had not darted out of the parking lot, we walked back and were on our way to the border. I sat in the middle of the front bench seat between a large Peruvian man and the driver who's gum chewing mouth smelled like Flintstone vitamins.

It is always a somewhat surreal experience to walk across the border of one country and into another. It is unfailingly interesting and perhaps feels more of an adventure than it really is for there is usually a change in landscape, people and culture at borders. Everyone's senses and sensibilities are heightened, and it is natural to be more aware and judgmental and compare how the border guards on one side treat you to how those on the other side do. In this case, both sides were pleasant enough in dealing with the busy line of locals and foreigners. But soon after leaving the border station inside Peru, the landscape was completely flat and covered in light-colored sand that stretched inland forever from the nearby ocean. There was nothing but sand. Not even a military outpost or a shack, just sand for miles and miles.

It was hard to believe the desert could become drier and hotter than it was in Chile, but it did, and it was accompanied by strong winds that occasionally shifted the course of our completely full taxi that barreled its way towards the uninspiring city of Tacna. The ocean could always be seen in the distance but through the desert's waves of heat it was a kind of glittering mirage that had a teasing presence.

There was little reason to stay in Tacna other than to stop for lunch and catch the bus to Arequipa. The roads from Tacna were as worrying as I thought they would be. It was unforgivingly hot as the bus traveled through the desert on roads that were at times nearly covered in sand. Tacna is at sea level and Arequipa is nearly four thousand feet up which meant there were a lot of steep inclines ahead of us. The roads are built into the cliffs and roughly finished on the edges giving the impression that they could give way at any time. It was clear that the roads have been built by dynamiting the sides of the mountains for there were huge chunks of rock that matched the mountains and only could have been moved with the help of explosives. Every turn was a harrowing experience for anyone paying attention. The front of the bus swung over the edge of a cliff and came too near to the edge of steep cliffs. Everyone was either sleeping or watching a terrible movie, oblivious to the potential disaster the driver nearly avoided at every turn.

When the road flattened out, we passed through small towns that were only a strip of the most basic structures alongside the road. The Peruvians sat tired and bored with their faces held in a supporting hand or resting their chin on a fist. Their stillness and the speed of the bus turned them into statues making the towns a sight of desperate boredom. They were odd places for there was nothing like crops to be found that needed to be tended to – these people were stranded in a desert beside the road as if they had broken down long ago and never got out. Some wore oversized cowboy hats that were as silly as cowboy hats always appear but they took on another dimension beneath such an oppressive sun – they were as necessary as helmets at a construction site. Even though the signs were advertisements, they looked like calls for help. I was relieved to see a nearby river, but it quickly disappeared.

We had gone further inland to climb up the mountains towards Arequipa and the ocean was no longer visible. It was only after passing piles of oddly colored sand that I realized what these little strip mall towns were for. Some piles of sand were a shiny silver and likely the result of some extraction plant or nearby mines. They successfully give the landscape an otherworldly dimension. Only did it become earthly with the sight of some ugly extraction plants in the distance.

I arrived in Arequipa at magic hour and could feel the effects from the altitude as we climbed up into the mountains and ultimately arrived at four thousand feet but the temperatures had pleasantly cooled even before it had gone completely dark and I no longer had to shield my eyes from the sun glaring off everything in the desert nor did I have to feel the oppressive heat that I now thought of in the same way as a patch of thorn bushes. Something that was inescapable.

Though, the altitude played with my head and I was tired from another long day of traveling through the heat, the beauty of Arequipa was hard to remove from the front of my mind, and I happily settled into the city.

13

Juanita

The first morning I walked onto the cobbled stone streets of Arequipa I had not expected to stare into the face of a young girl who had died five hundred years earlier. In a cool dark room of the Museo Santuarios Andinos the remains of a mummy were on display. It was an unassuming place that I had stumbled upon without any previous knowledge. The museum was devoted to the preservation of Incan artifacts mostly found in the mountains around Arequipa. The young girl had obviously died many centuries earlier, but it had only recently been concluded that she had died of less than natural causes.

I was soon eye to eye socket with her skull covered in dried skin giving it a horrifyingly purgatorial expression to the rest of the shrunken frame. The age of the girl upon death was around fourteen, but now shriveled to the size of a child of about four years and sat up in a position known as, 'seat-flex,' that looked as though her arms pulled her knees to her chest. The body had shrunk significantly over time from the loss of fluids even though the bone structure, much of the skin, and hair were well preserved. It became a stark reminder as to how much of a human body is made up of liquid. The cloth wrapped loosely around the skeleton made the body seem more a mannequin than a mummy.

Mummy Juanita, as she has come to be called, is sat inside a climate-controlled tank so as to properly preserve her body which had been preserved in the ground for over five hundred years. Now, out in the open she was much more vulnerable to the elements of a room in a museum. Struggling to preserve her remains was nothing new once she had been discovered. Even though it was a dead body behind a glass case, it was set in as much of a throne like position as possible for this was not just any dead body, but one of the most well-preserved mummies to be found in the Andes by Johan Reinhard.

Reinhard has had a prolific career of climbing throughout the Andes and discovering dozens of lost Incan burial sites. The discovery of Juanita was not only one of the most significant finds but the trek itself proved memorably difficult, and Reinhard and his crew struggled to complete the journey.

The trek to find her was an arduous one and even though much work was done to put Reinhard and his crew in the vicinity of some Incan sacrificial sites, it was only do to a chance spotting of some grass on the side of the mountain that had appeared after some ice had melted away. The arduous trek and the chance find of Juanita were mere precursors to the dramatic race back down the mountain to Arequipa with the frozen corpse. With the body frozen all the way through it meant there was a chance for the first time to extract preserved organs from a female sacrificial specimen for DNA testing.

Reinhard and his trekking partner Miki struggled and suffered physically to trek back down the mountain amidst the altitude, cold weather and rocky terrain. Falling numerous times their bodies took a beating in order to return with the mummy in the best possible shape. Miki regularly pleaded with Reinhard to leave the mummy and return for it the next day when the weather was not as harsh. But a determined Reinhard refused time and again. Miki grew increasingly scared that not only would Reinhard hurt himself but could potentially fall on him with his large pack and send them both plummeting down the mountain. The physical strain soon took its toll and they were forced to leave the mummy for the night and made their way to the relative safety and shelter of their camp. The next day, somewhat rested, they retrieved the body and continued to descend.

Further down where they had the help of another trekking partner, Henri, and a few donkeys to carry their packs and Juanita, and proceeded to trek for more than half a day before reaching a small town where an overnight bus could take them to Arequipa. The whole time they were hoping to escape the eyes of the police who would likely confiscate everything for they had no archaeological permits. They eventually made it to a friend's house in Arequipa and put the mummy in his oversized freezer.

The discovery of Juanita became a media event and further expeditions were planned to excavate more sights on Mount Ampato. In the next two years a few more mummies were discovered on the mountain.

The day I visited Mummy Juanita, there were no large crowds but the few visitors in the dimly lit rooms of the museum displayed a kind of awestruck worship to the little shrunken frame set before them in a climate-controlled case. It was unsurprising for Mummy Juanita was not merely just a miraculous scientific specimen but still considered a religious symbol of sorts. A common aspect of many faiths across the world is an emphasis on purity, derived from both virginity and youth, and the Incas were no different than many other religious cultures in selecting children to be sacrificed for this very reason. However, Inca culture allowed each sacrificed child to become a kind of God in and of themselves and were worshiped on a similar plain as the mountain Gods, making it an honor to be sacrificed as well as an honor for the parents. Child sacrifice was done as a reciprocal gesture to the Gods for all they had given to people on earth. It was also done in the hope that the Gods would stop natural disasters, such as the volcanic eruptions and earthquakes that had occurred from time to time.

Those children that climbed the mountains for these sacrificial ceremonies including Juanita and the three other children found on the mountain, were ultimately marching to their deaths. Reinhard's descriptions of the difficulties of the treks, makes the ascent of the mountains all those centuries ago seem an even more extreme event. They were brave and persistent travelers and likely determined out of a spiritual responsibility to reach the peak of the mountain. Reinhard and his crew were professional climbers and it is mind boggling to think of those young children climbing the mountain five hundred years ago with equipment that could only be described as primitive.

It has been concluded that Juanita's death was the result of child sacrifice as a part of local Inca custom. It was also concluded that Juanita died by a blow to the head with some kind of club or mallet, determined by the presence of a cracked skull.

Spiritual connection with the mountains and the surrounding lands remains with the locals centuries later for one of Reinhard's fellow trekkers, a Peruvian, said, "for us the mountains are alive." The Peruvians believe the mountains are living. Peruvians are close to the land in nearly every way and it's no surprise they would not only come to look upon the land for purposes of imperial power and agricultural prosperity but also see it through a kind of spiritual prism. The area around Arequipa is volatile in that the land makes its own kind of noise and movements through volcanic eruptions and earthquakes. The earth is just as alive as are human beings and it is difficult to see otherwise when there are half a dozen volcanoes erupting all around you and the earth starts to shake.

I was not interested in climbing any mountains or descending into canyons, I preferred the activity surrounding Arequipa's churches and cathedrals. There was more life in the people than there ever could be in the most volatile of earthquakes. The altitude of Arequipa's flat streets was enough of a climb for me and I felt no spiritual connection with the land. Its cathedral was an intriguing building because of its massive organ from Belgium and one of its side chapels was graced with the presence of a black Jesus. The cathedral had fallen victim to a earthquake a few years earlier, its bell tower came crashing down onto the roof.

From the happy atmosphere of Arequipa's churches and squares the surrounding mountains looked a menacing presence and after spending some time learning about Mummy Juanita and what it had taken to go all that way just to sacrifice those children atop those treacherous peaks, the faith of the Incas looked as cruel as any other. Much of what tourists hear in the stories concerning the Inca empire is in the tragedy and cruelty of their fall at the hands of the Spanish. But there was no foreign army marching behind Juanita or behind the Inca men that marched behind her. Their cruelty was born out of their own superstition. Cruelty does not live in any one race, culture or religion - it is a human trait. The human sacrifices made by the Incas are evidence of their own cruelty towards one another and proof they had more respect for their land and Gods than their fellow human beings.

As I sat in the main square of the city I thought of the visitors from Australia, the United States, and the United Kingdom who naturally looked at Mummy Juanita with awe, and treated her as a Christlike figure to be respected for what she represented and had been sacrificed for rather than for what she was, a child. These tourists, some young but mostly old, who shared a wide mouth expression at how well preserved her body was were quickly consumed with the aura of her body. They were ready to pray, ready to go native, so to speak. I had been silently condemning the cruelty of the Incas towards their young, but I thought that if these distant foreigners could not resist the pull of this mountainous faith, how could the Incas?

Mummy Juanita's sacrifice has unsurprisingly proved futile for the volcanic eruptions still came, as did the earthquakes, as did the poverty, the hunger and ultimately the suffering in the mountains and valleys of Peru. Mummy Juanita was not merely a well-preserved body of a young girl, but she proved to be one of the consequences of another disreputable faith. A faith that would argue that the eruptions, earthquakes and suffering would be quelled, and the Gods satisfied were there more Juanitas. Superstition is a part of life in Peru and always has been. Whether the Gods were thought to exist in the earth or in the sky brought from conquerors of a distant land, there was always a willingness to worship in Peru.

14

Arequipa

At the top of the Basilica Catedral de Arequipa the three volcanoes surrounding the city Misti, Chachani, and Pichu Pichu, slept like menacing giants. Earthquakes were also always a potential menace to the city and have ravaged and destroyed the cathedral on more than one occasion. The large bell tower I stood next to had fallen over onto the roof from the last earthquake more than a decade earlier which had a magnitude of 8.4 on the Richter scale.

Below the cathedral in the Plaza de Armas was the celebration of the 471st anniversary of the city of Arequipa. Crowds were coming and going and a tent and platform for speakers was set up at the bottom of the plaza but most everyone was waiting around for the celebration to kick-off, though it was being held up by some local politicians who were supposed to deliver speeches. Hundreds of Peruvian soldiers separated into several different units marched around the cobble stoned streets of the plaza eventually coming to a halt where they baked in the dry heat. One was an urban unit of tall expressionless men with large shotguns fit with silencers and Tommy-Gun clips, while another unit entirely made up of short men in khaki desert uniforms with backpacks and round turtle shell helmets carried M16s. Other units each outfitted in a different uniform and tactical weaponry looked as though they were each assigned to a particular region of the country.

A handful of snipers stood on the roofs of the buildings bordering the plaza, surveying the crowds with the barrel of the rifle held close to a cheek.

A procession of teenage girls lined up on a side street leading into the plaza and was part of a larger band that stretched further down the street. Dressed in large white cowboy hats, navy blue blazers, red and yellow striped belts, black ties, curved collared buttoned up shirts, plaid blue skirts, navy blue socks pulled up to the shins, and flat black shoes with a buckle and strap. On the street beside them were a long line of more teenage girls dressed like cheerleaders in tight white dresses and white cowboy hats who practiced twirling batons.

The plaza had the air of a spectacle that is found in small Texan towns before football games or homecoming ceremonies. There were plenty of tourists and other idlers in the city left to watch, but it still felt like everyone wanted to be in the ceremony. Far too many people were on display.

I grew tired of waiting for the ceremonies to begin and walked away from the main square towards the Iglesia de San Francisco. Arequipa is dry and the altitude that plays with the brain of those coming from Lima or Northern Chile makes the grid city feel like a baffling maze further complicated by the bustle of the main plaza. The light of the sun is particularly strong and puts a strain on the eyes. I stopped in the monastery along the way to be covered by its cool shaded rooms.

I attended mass nearly every day at one of Arequipa's churches or the main cathedral. Each church had an overwhelming amount of detail. If there was not a plethora of gold there was intricate stonework that covered nearly every inch of space. Much of the area in and around the main plaza of the city was dotted with these detailed stone structures to which and from flowed currents of worshippers. Some evening services were filled to the walls with locals, so full the capacity of each pew was completely stretched and those who were late had to stand in the aisles, any open space or even out the front doors. Other services were small and consisted of mostly foreigners and tourists easily distinguished by the colors and materials of their clothing. Women were brought to the front to tell emotional stories crying throughout while consoled by the nearby priest. Babies cried and children ran to and fro on the carpeted aisle. Nighttime services were often close to dark with a few lights and prayer candles to illuminate the service.

I had not been in the smaller church attached to Iglesia de San Francisco. I wandered in from the nearby plaza during noon mass expecting to find the walls echoing with the faint sounds of afternoon worshippers fidgeting in the pews, but was greeted by a completely full service. I weaved my way through to the other side near a large medieval door one step below the main floor. There was an entire pew of elderly men each missing a leg from the mid-thigh down. The missing legs wore shortened pant legs carefully tailored and folded without a cuff, while beside them were small wooden crutches.

As the service neared its end the Altar boys arranged the pews creating a line along the walls of the church leading to a large door where I was standing a step down from the main level. A long set of instructions from the priest went unnoticed by the people rushing for the door and a crowd quickly formed. No one tried to open it or go through, for it was understood that the Altar boys must open the door. They still rushed for the best position, but at the speed of very elderly people which was more determined by the wideness of their eyes rather than the speed of their feet, which changed very little. Their rugged faces were made young as they pushed and shoved like children, quickly becoming impatient and making every possible move to get in front of one another.

Little old ladies in homemade sweaters who charged towards the small landing were shrunk to their real heights as they came down the one step. They were all under four foot ten and weighed no more than a hundred pounds, the tops of their heads coming up to my chest or just above the elbow. Their short stature made them seem even poorer than they already looked, and their homemade clothes spotted with patches, wrapped each one of them in humility. None of them appeared to have dwarfism, they all seemed simply small from something like in-breeding. It could not be that they were all the runt of their families, but that they came from small people who came from small people.

As the landing became full, I was slowly pushed against the wall, and there was the anticipation of the crowd becoming a manic force, but in truth there was little to fear because of how small they were. I looked into their impatient faces as they jostled for position closer to the door, and began to panic merely because the person next to them was doing so. Each face was filled with the worry that they might not get through the door. It was the sort of mania that has the potential to infect all crowds. Whoever bumped into me bounced back into the crowd like a pinball and I put my hands up to catch the little bodies that were slowly pressed against mine. One woman fell into me and I caught her by the back of the ribs which were as frail as the sweater she wore. She tried repeatedly to get through the crowd but was continually shoved back into me and time after time I softened her fall and prevented her from hitting the wall, each time I caught her, her ribs felt more like those of a hummingbird I held in my hand.

Age was irrelevant to the one-legged man who came storming from behind like a young protester, shouting and then pushed into the crowd with his chest and head, the homemade crutches firmly planted into the church floor. I had recognized his energized face from when I walked past him as he sat in the pew. The scrum of people easily absorbed his light frame and he was eventually swept further into the crowd like a stick caught in an undertow. Their collective impatience made for a constant change in each person's position and a heightening of the panic. The way to survive the crowd was to panic along with everyone else which was apparent to the worshippers who were quickly filled with the fear of being the only person not panicking. Arguments broke out over nothing and as they grew more heated, I gazed up at the ornate ceiling covered in gold and the beautifully carved stone walls calmly looking down on all of us. None of the people looked up at the walls or ceilings of the church, it meant little to them. Crucifixes hung motionless from the walls and the dead bodies of Christ were like curious onlookers.

A mildly retarded woman with a body like an old pear stood a foot away from the door, staring and confused as to how to open it. She was nearly my height and thus much taller than everyone around her making her look lost and out of place, perhaps like me. She had emerged at the front of the crowd and some of the little old ladies were not pleased by this fact. A small clique became more irritated by the slow woman and began to badger her, making sharp quips and pointing their bent fingers at her. The slow woman was more confused than frightened or startled by the women hounding her. They all barked. Everyone was barking at one another, but they could be easily swatted away like feathers if necessary. One, in a homemade button-up purple sweater and a long skirt kept up the badgering after the rest had quieted down and was only slightly pacified when an Altar boy arrived at the door, and while slowly pushing his palm towards the floor, said, "Tranquilo, Señora, tranquilo." It merely lessened the amount she said, but she still seethed at the slow woman. Some of the other ladies held her back.

They were all too close to the door for it to open completely, but as the door began to open, the sounds of excitement jumped out of their bodies and suddenly room was made for it to open completely as the crowd shifted itself and rushed through the doorway. I was still unsure what the line was for and was too busy watching the crowd to suspect anything other than a continuation of the service in some way. Their thin frames made me conscious of how much bigger I was, how much healthier I was, and one small lady asked me if I wanted to get in front of her when the door began to open. I told her I should let more people go ahead of me as there was quite a buildup behind us including a few people in wheelchairs, besides, I had no clue what this line was for or where it was leading to.

The doorway led us out of the church into the hallway outdoors that cut into another dark hallway. We then made another slow turn and I could see people handing out plates next to large cooking pots. Seeing that it was a line for food, it was enough to make any recently fed person feel ridiculous and out of place. I imagined an Altar boy quietly taking me by the hand and escorting me to the exit and politely pointing towards a restaurant, where people able to pay are meant to eat. I felt overly nourished and clearly not in need of food, everyone around me was old and poor, blind, or cripple. When I thought of getting out of the line, I looked down at the old faces which looked back at me with mischievous grins over the excitement that we would all be eating lunch soon. Their faces told me to get a plate before they were all gone. A woman with a soft smile gave me a big bowl of rice, potatoes, vegetables and Alpaca soup while another woman gave me a cup pomegranate juice. After receiving my food there was a courtyard in front of me where all were eating happily and chatting away. It was touching to be eating with all of them, I felt privileged to receive a plate. I felt out of place, but it was no fault of the people around me, just mine, they were still kind to me.

An old man excitedly came up to me and spoke in inaudible Spanish full of slang. He pulled on my arm for me to join him where he was sitting with other elderly men and women. They looked at me like they had known me for a hundred years even though they had only known me for a few minutes. We could not understand one another but were satisfied by our attempts to do so. We all smiled in the sun-drenched courtyard and together we ate Alpaca soup.

15

Puno

I had quickly fallen in love with the city of Arequipa and was sad to leave its bevy of churches and princely plaza. The city had the royal air of a small principality. It was a small country on a hill or more precisely a valley surrounded by volcanoes. But I felt like moving on and that meant moving further up the mountains towards Lake Titicaca. The roads took on the same shape as the ones from Tacna to Arequipa but were steeper and at much higher altitudes. Every mile that went by ascended to a greater altitude which would bring forth increasingly difficult conditions. The difference in altitude from Arequipa to Puno was eight thousand feet and the ride that was a manageable time of five to six hours only felt longer with every thousand feet higher the bus climbed. The highest I had ever been in my life was ten thousand feet which I had gone to after a week spent at five thousand feet. Now, to go from Arequipa to Puno in five or six hours was an extreme change I was unprepared for and would feel immediately.

Lake Titicaca looked a surreal and soothing sight in the distance but with my rapidly growing headache that resisted any medicine other than descending it was not as soothing as I hoped. Again, I arrived in another Peruvian city at twilight, but Puno quickly became even more unforgiving for the temperature dropped below freezing shortly after dark. I was cold, dizzy and by the time I climbed the stairs to my room on the third floor after dinner I was out of breath. It was not long before I began to worry about what the altitude might do to me in my sleep, but I had little other option than to go to bed and see how I felt the next morning.

I awoke rested but still with a slight headache and hoped some fresh air and a little journey on the lake would cure me. By midday Puno would come to show another one of its unforgiving traits and that was the strong glare of its sun and its dry mouth inducing thin air. Puno looked pleasant enough, but it was difficult to enjoy for every one of its natural elements was after you in some way.

The floating islands were intriguing enough to trek down the dock and onto a rickety boat towards the center of the lake. After all the desert and mountains there was now a lake, a very large one that straddles the borders of Peru and Bolivia. It is the highest lake in the world and the residents of its floating islands had some of the sternest faces a person could possibly have. The women were large with broad shoulders, thick legs and leathery skin. Their facial expressions rarely shifted whether they were joking with tourists or maneuvering one of the home-made boats docked beside the islands. They were so androgynous looking, and had they not been wearing the long colorful skirts that nearly all women wear in the mountains of Peru they could have easily been mistaken for men. Their thick frames and ambiguous faces somehow sent my mind into the gutter and I was doing my best to imagine their sex lives, more for some kind of cultural clarity rather than personal pleasure. But even mentally walking in such a world inevitably leads one towards the curiosity of what it would be like to spend an evening with such a lady, for they had an extreme look that could easily be considered a fetish for some Wall Street banker to secretly indulge in. They were the opposite of everything I thought to be sexually attractive and sometimes one notices what they are not attracted to just as much as what they are attracted to. Momentarily, one inevitably thinks they could be missing out on something. I did, too, but not for long because this short mental sojourn I embarked on whilst sitting in the middle of Lake Titicaca proved all too fruitless for rarely is it possible to vividly imagine people you are not attracted to in a sexualized state.

The floating islands were an amusing sight for so is most anything that floats. Built mostly of tall reeds plucked from the lake and tightly packed earth it was a surprise to feel just how durable they were when walking on them.

My interest in the islands soon wavered as there proved little to do after a half hour or so and the islands looked more like a gimmicky tourist trap rather than an enduring local custom. I was still reeling from the effects of the altitude and it was not long before I was struggling back up the stairs to my bed. I was meant to stay three more days but impulsively went down to the train station and bought a ticket for the tourist train down to Cusco in the morning.

I was the first at the station the next morning but was quickly joined by a few hundred boisterous tourists from all over the western world. I thought the small pack of tourists on the floating island and the few wandering backpackers in the streets were the only foreigners in Puno, but I now realized there was always an abundance of tourists in nearly every corner of Peru no matter how distant or sparsely populated a place appeared. I was excited to be heading towards Cusco and further on to Machu Picchu as were the others who filled the little hall to board the train. I was doubly excited to be descending to a more reasonable nine thousand feet, where I hoped my headache would subside and I could get back to enjoying the life of the country.

The noise of the tourists only grew when we boarded the train, and there was a chaotic half-hour of trying to fit an excessive amount of bags into compartments and shooing people out of the wrong seats before we pushed away from the station. The car was filled with the most unhappy families 'holidaying' in Peru, seemingly as one large organism. The families were of several nationalities but shared more than just a pink cheeked complexion. The children of a British family fought with each other, whining incessantly about the littlest of things. They were all embarrassed by their 'Hooray Harry' father. One of the sons kept shouting, "Dad! Dad! Dad!" whenever the father became unbearably embarrassing. The father was ignorant of not only everything around him, but of his kids, too. They asked questions of how to work apps on their phones or how to get batteries into a camera or some other device. Struggling with the smallest of tasks, I worried with potential shame at the possibility of some Peruvians walking through the car and witnessing this embarrassingly low display of acumen, class, and capability amongst so many Americans and Europeans. I pondered the technical ease with which Peruvians labored in the streets and fields. Some of these teenage girls ended up in full blown crying fits, doing their best with the direction of one of their parents to hold in the noise as much as possible, but it could easily be heard from the other end of the car. We were going the same place and they had seven times more stuff than I did. I wondered what could be in all of those bags.

I sat facing the same direction the train headed and got to experience the change in landscape as we chugged along towards the Sacred Valley. Across the aisle from me were two older couples from New Rochelle, New York. We smiled and laughed at being in such a far-flung place yet coming from more or less the same place.

"We are American Jews," they said, when the subject quickly made its way to Israel. Each couple had a son in the IDF and spoke proudly of it. George was an accountant, and Larry was in marketing and their conversation was of Israeli and American politics with more agreement on the former than the latter. There was a discussion of the things they would accept for a certain bill to be passed. They spoke in tired political clichés and each little term or phrase sounded duller than the last. Words like spending, security, budget, administration, and policy brought forth images of bureaucratic boredom from a distant culture that did not involve going through deserts and mountains. These were inside words meant for places with dark green rugs and flickering tube lights. They had a spoiling effect just like the bratty kids at the other end of the car. I had rarely heard such words in the past couple of months and hearing them in the confines of a train car only meant I would have to keep on hearing them for a few hours. Other than inspire boredom it made me aware of how distant I was from that sort of life and how wayward an existence I was living. But I was in the same expensive train car as them going the same place, and I grew up only a few miles from where they did. Everyone comes through Peru, I suppose. They were nice enough, but the potential for argument was perched on their lips, and I did my best to stray from any disagreements as I did not want the ride to become longer than it already was. I did my best to avoid the political discussions and was thankful for the presence of their pretty wives, who each sat beside them displaying both poise and patience and were more interested in talking to me than their husbands.

Both were blonde, beautiful and pleasantly named Aviva and Ora. The wives were more impressive than the husbands. They spoke little, not for lack of something to say but for saying less was a trait of someone in possession of class and style. Brevity turns out to be the soul of style, too. The men were the chatty ones and said too much. When they were not discussing US domestic spending they were fiddling with high powered cameras, struggling to twist on and off oversized lenses. Often taking pictures of random things; sometimes down the aisle of the train car or at the side of a mountain.

Everyone shifted around their seats to break up the monotony during the long journey. The men continued the policy debate, Ora got lost in a book and Aviva took the seat across from me. We happily spoke of trivial things and enjoyed each other's company. This was the fastest and most direct route to Cusco, while the bus was supposedly a nauseating ride down the mountains and was a few hours longer. Here was someone from fifteen minutes from where I grew up. Together we watched the poor people dotting the fields and mountains like colorful bushes laboriously tilling away at the earth. Their lives were world's away from those of the people inside the train car. Fires burned in hay fields a few hundred yards from the tracks and by the time we reached Cusco all the light in the sky had gone.

16

Sacred Valley

I was relieved to be at the lower altitude of nine thousand feet and away from the arduousness of every step one takes in Puno. It does not take long to realize that Cusco is a kind of crossroads and a peculiar one at that for its distance from everywhere on earth. It is not a trade route nor a nexus of countries or continents but purely a tourist crossroads. Visitors travel from the furthest of distances to this city in the Sacred Valley, but Cusco and the valley are also a unique crossroads to its bordering regions, surrounded by jungle, desert and everything to the west; a long downwards slide towards Lima and the Pacific Ocean.

There were plenty of Americans and Brits and Australians bustling about while French, Italian and German could be heard in almost every restaurant or hotel lobby. There were so many foreigners that the Peruvians looked an outnumbered minority. The city was entrenched in the dealings of the modern traveler yet remained steadfast and immovable. Cusco is somehow aesthetically pleasing even though it rarely exhibits anything other than a few shades of dark brown stone. Just like the ruined sites of the Sacred Valley, it is of the earth and resembles a kind of castle.

I was not bothered by the presence of so many familiar cultures, for it felt as though everyone was there for some monumental once in a lifetime event. It was obvious of course. There was the feeling of the night before, an anticipation before a great event. That exciting something was Machu Picchu.

The foreigners are a constant fixture of the city and as transient as they actually are, they appear in a way pinned down or settled. Similar in that way to Bangkok where a regular flow of white red cheeked faces exists amongst those of the locals.

Were the city not at the edge of or the jumping off point for exploring the Sacred Valley it would still stand as great, but it is inevitably a Medina to Machu Picchu's Mecca.

Most travelers I spoke with arrived overland from Lima and therefore arrived sick from a treacherous cliff-climbing bus ride and from zip-lining the altitude from sea level to nine thousand feet. More than once I found myself overhearing someone on the phone to a family member back home explaining how sick they were from the altitude and the bus ride. I was at an advantage to have descended to Cusco and acclimated to the city with less trouble. The air only seemed fresher and more breathable even if it was slightly dirtier. I had done most of the acclimating I needed. Rest and time were not the sole method for dealing with the effects of altitude, for everywhere there was some form of coca leaves being sold as a short-term cure for headaches and shortness of breath. Old ladies on the street sold little plastic bags full of them while they chewed on a cheek-full of leaves. Cafes brewed the leaves into tea and corner stores sold them in the form of candies and gums. I bought a bag of leaves and drank a coca tea and quickly felt relaxed and my small lingering headache had soon gone. The high that comes from coca leaves is minimal but effective in combating altitude.

That first night I drank two more mugs of tea and chewed the rest of the leaves while walking around Cusco late into the night. There were more than a few drug dealers in the streets and even in a pizza place decorated with reggae flags and hippy paraphernalia, the old dreadlocked Peruvian owner looking like Cusco's own Tommy Chong, openly offered drugs to me and other tourists. It seemed a risky thing to be doing, and even a risk to be around. I refused, for I was not interested, and other travelers had given me strong warnings to avoid any and all drugs solely because of the punishment of a Peruvian jail. There is no getting out of jail in Peru, no matter what one has or has not done.

The next morning, I woke up with what I thought to be a hangover from the coca leaves but was more a return of the altitude headaches after the slight effects of the leaves had worn off in the night. I knew I had had too much and that I would have to use them sparingly so as not to trick my brain into thinking the altitude had completely gone.

The tea became my preferred method of consuming coca, for the leaves were a mess, and the candies were mixed with far too much sugar which made for an odd cocktail.

****

After a few days I was settled into the city and eager to explore the wider valley, but whilst continuing to acclimate I spent a great deal of time reflecting on the cities I had just come from. Peruvian culture was much more significant than that of Chile and there were far more people. It was in no way aggressive, but you were confronted with its bold presence.

Arequipa was a society unto itself and Puno was a quiet place and also so jarring from the altitude that I could hardly get a sense of its culture. I only realized how significant a history and culture this part of the earth contained when I got to Cusco. The city and the Sacred Valley make one shamefully aware of how ignorant they often are to the long and storied history of the Incas and their land. I had not gone

173

through the front door to Cusco as most visitors do from Lima, but I now hoped that this sort of entrée would only further my curiosity.

In an odd way, it was a pleasure to know nothing about a culture, to be confronted with a blank slate, and be able to vividly remember when you started to read and learn about it. Most every store sold a number of books on the history of the Incas and explorers who came centuries after they had fallen. There was naturally Hiram Bingham's account of 'discovering' Machu Picchu and then Hugh Thomas' *The White Rock,* which looked at other lost sights in the valley. But none was more intriguing or as thorough as the complete history carefully sewn together by John Hemming's *'The Conquest of the Incas.'* Partially an answer to William Prescott's *'The Conquest of Peru,'* Hemming succeeds where Prescott did in showcasing the Spanish side of the conquest and also where he did not which was in showcasing the perspective of the Incas, mainly its rulers whose divided state and ultimately unsuccessful attempts to fend off the Spanish invaders proved the end of the empire. It is a monumental book about an equally monumental civilization.

The time before the arrival of the Spanish is still shrouded in darkness. Without the specifics one could imagine that the previous century or two of the Inca empire before the arrival of the Spanish was none too different than the one the Spanish encountered. A likely difference was that the empire itself was more united and tightly controlled by previous Inca rulers.

Since much of what is known about the Incas is through the tragic stories of the fall of its rulers, its history is shrouded with an imperial flavor. This taste for the monarchical is only further enhanced by the grand sites of the Sacred Valley. All of the stone palaces dotted around the valley are the desires of kings, they are royal in character and never cease to be grand, yet they are the labors of the common man and woman, either enslaved or faithful to their kings.

While getting my bearings of the city and eager for a view of it, I naturally found myself walking up the hill towards the almost illusory Sacsayhuaman, a truly magnificent sight, made with incredibly large boulders. As much as one may struggle, it is nearly impossible to fathom the human effort it took to haul such large rocks to form the neatly constructed fortress atop the hill overlooking the city. Even in 'ruins' it still remains an unbreakable site, making it more difficult to fathom the defeat the Incas and their thousands of soldiers and ordinary citizens succumbed to at the hands of less than two hundred Spanish soldiers. Having already read the story of the Spanish siege of the city and the fateful role Sacsayhuaman played in this battle between thousands of Incan soldiers and citizens and a mere one hundred and sixty Spanish soldiers on horseback, it was all the more a sensational sight. The peaceful bustle of a few hundred tourists were dwarfed by its immensity. The story fresh in my mind, I easily imagined the dramatic and lopsided victory, and this site was the beginning of the end of the Inca empire.

Contrary to popular belief the conquest of the Incas did not start with a mass invasion of the empire's long Pacific coastline, that would happen later. The first Spanish intrusions into Incan territory had come from the north by way of modern-day Ecuador and Colombia. Once the conflicts between the Spaniards and the Incas started, the powers within the Inca kingdom began to shift and smallpox did much of the initial fighting for the Spanish conquerors. The disease killed hundreds and then thousands of Incas throughout the kingdom, including its then ruler Huayna Capac and his supposed heir Ninan Coyoche. Since Huayna Capac's affairs were out of order there was no established line of succession and no designated heir. It goes to show how off guard the Incas were to Spanish invasion, but it also shows how fragile the Inca empire and its power structure were to begin with. The Spanish were toppling the Incas without even seeing them. The Incas were also used to local and regional wars against tribes who were even less technologically advanced than themselves.

The death of the Inca ruler and his heir immediately created a power struggle and a war between his next two sons who were known for little else than their penchant for surfing the Pacific coastline. At the time of the Spaniard's arrival the Incas were becoming increasingly divided. The brothers, Atahuallpa and Huascar, were no longer resigned to the leisurely days of third and fourth in line to the throne but were consumed with ambition that plunged the Inca kingdom into civil war. Atahuallpa would eventually prevail over Huascar and this was the first ruler that the Spaniards would come to make contact with. Therefore, not only did the Spaniards receive help in conquering the natives through biological means, but through the help of the natives themselves. The subsequent leadership and inevitable deaths of the following Inca rulers would take their own unique shape. The Incas did the dividing, the Spaniards the conquering and once they established a grip on power, the Spanish never ceased to further divide the Incas.

Reading of these divisions amongst the ruling classes made me somewhat disappointed and to a degree I looked upon this inner turmoil of the Incas as a reinforcement of that simplistic and cliché tactic of divide and conquer that has ushered in the fall of so many civilizations. It was indicative of the folly of human nature and man's capacity to let a good thing go bad. These cities and their stones looked unbreakable, but I came to see that a true empire is something other than hard rock laden structures. Without unity, its castles and monuments and even its achievements are naught.

Perhaps the Inca empire would have had a chance had it had a military that was equally modern as the Spanish but in hindsight it appears a hopeless fight considering that the small Spanish force was led by the maniacal Francisco Pizarro and his band of crazed brothers.

Pizarro like most conquistadors, was in possession of an almost uncontrollable ambition. He learned from Cortés and idolized his exploits in Mexico, seeking to find his own Mexico along the little explored Pacific coastline of South America which was ripe for plundering. Pizarro was obsessed with gold and land and later with young Inca women. Power for Pizarro was more or less a given for there was never any considerable struggle within his own forces as the top commanding positions were occupied by his ever-loyal brothers. Challenges from within would come later.

Being a force of less than two hundred the Spanish were in a wilderness when facing an empire of thousands of Inca soldiers and citizens. There was little time or reason to struggle for power because Pizarro and his men almost equally shared in the bloody fighting that ensued. Spanish ambitions were truly quixotic in nature but became all the more reasonable to achieve when they learned what kind of force they were up against.

****

As much as has been painstakingly unearthed from the largely unwritten times of the Incas and uncovered beneath the green claws of the jungle, there is still much mystery surrounding the life and society of the Incas. Without a written language and relying on an antiquated rope knot system whereby the number of knots tied into long ropes have certain meanings for specific events over centuries, generally, stories were verbally passed on.

From the information that has made its way to the present and recorded in the early days of the conquest, it is a certainty that it was a brutal time in more than one respect.

Life before the arrival of the Spanish was doubtlessly difficult for the less privileged classes and generally any woman was at risk of becoming some kind of slave to the Inca ruler himself or one of his inner circle. Slavery was rife between local tribes and death often settled arguments amongst locals where there was no other solution deemed possible. Compared to today it would be considered a brutal time, and those lower rungs of the society's ladder suffered far more than those nearer the top. But after the arrival of the Spanish, the upper echelons of Inca society and most of the Inca rulers themselves, became full-fledged targets of the Spanish. They were obvious targets for the power they held and control they had over the rest of the empire. Like any monarchical symbol their longevity or decline would determine the rest of the empire's fate.

Each Inca ruler suffered defeat often in a dramatic and unique manner, but none was more prolonged and dramatic than that of Manco. He had initially collaborated with the Spanish to sew up power and protection from any internal enemies, but quickly started to rebel against the Spaniards, mobilizing large armed forces engaged in guerrilla warfare against them.

Manco eventually had some of the Spaniards invited to visit him in Cusco so that he could get a better sense of these foreigners. Awaiting them, Manco had made sure lots of gold and silver plates and bowls were on display to show how wealthy he and his empire were. The gold obsessed Spaniards quickly convinced Manco to let them 'borrow' some of the gold and silver items to take back to Cajamarca and Lima to show their compatriots the greatness of his power and how wealthy an empire he ruled over.

Manco's vanity and stupidity would have long lasting consequences for the fate of the empire and provide the Spaniards with a consistent weakness to exploit. The Spaniards accused Manco of planning an uprising against their control. The Spaniards were obviously greed ridden conquerors who had no interest in a true partnership with the Incas, but Manco was far too naive of a leader who sought to please and appease the Spaniards at every step. The Spaniards were thieves and murderers who only could have seen the empire's treasures as something easily obtained with a man like Manco in charge. Manco made the mistake of letting the Spaniards further into the inner kingdom. He let a foreign force close to him and gave access that put his safety at their mercy and therefore the fate of the kingdom as well. Manco was taken captive and Pizarro proceeded to shake down Manco for all the gold he could. The Pizarro brothers demanded he get as much gold and silver as possible from his subjects. Manco made a speech to a large crowd of Incas and said he would be released if the treasure was collected.

The Pizarro brothers were wicked even by the standards of other conquistadors. Though, of all of the brothers, Gonzalo Pizarro was a truly deviant soul. A beast of a man, who needed no instruction from his own king or nasty brothers in how to be brutal to those who stepped in his path. The demands for gold and silver continued and when a confidant of Manco's objected to the demands of supplying more, he was met with a tirade from Gonzalo: "Who has commanded you to speak with such authority to the Corregidor of the King? Do you have any idea what sort of people we Spaniards are? You had better be quiet! Otherwise, I'll swear by the life of his Majesty that if I get a hold of you, I will teach you and your companions a lesson that you'll remember for the rest of your life. If you won't shut up, I swear that I'll burn you alive and hack you to pieces. Who has ordered him, I ask to speak with such air before me?" He continued, "you had better stop this and hurry together the silver and gold, as I have ordered you. Otherwise, I swear to you that your king will not leave this prison until everything has been gathered, even if it takes a year. So stop arguing with me and don't tell me any stories about your rank deeds, from here he went, and from over there he came."

The efforts made to free Manco were futile and almost laughably passive. Pleading with the vastly more powerful and aggressive Spaniards, Inca chief Vila Oma pleaded with the Spaniards to let their king go. It was only when a great deal of gold and silver were finally delivered to the Spanish that he was freed.

Manco's naivety would prove fatal, and his ignorance continually blinded him to what he was up against. After each humiliating shake-down he proved to be passive in the face of these foreign invaders. When Gonzalo Pizarro, who felt he had not been given a fair share in the first shakedown, went back to Manco and accused him of deception against him and his brothers, and conspiring an uprising, he demanded more gold and silver. Instead of ordering a full-scale revolt, Manco had his subject's spend two months gathering as much silver and gold as possible. When Manco was told that all the silver had been collected Gonzalo Pizarro demanded another treasure, Manco's sister. Manco tried to hand over several different women before handing over Ynguill, a friend of his sister, whom Gonzalo was eventually satisfied with.

Manco was again taken prisoner. Manco seemingly confused, and now feeling as though he were simply being fooled with, he had no choice but to capitulate to his powerful jailer. The entire process of rounding up more gold and silver was repeated before Manco was released again.

When Manco thought peace had been achieved through these ransoms, the Spaniards accused him a third time of an uprising. During an Inca festival the Spaniards stole more gold and silver from the Incas. Manco finally assembled all his chiefs in Cusco and had them send as many soldiers to the city in order to battle the Spaniards. A fighting force of over 400,000 Incas surrounded the Spaniards. The soldiers were ordered not to attack but ultimately harassed the Spaniards while awaiting Manco's arrival in Cusco. This was to become the dramatic battle of Sacsayhuaman. The Spaniards made a break for it thus disorganizing the Incas who made chase. The Spaniards took Sacsahuayman, the battle lasting three days and then aggressively counterattacked. There were even Incas on their side including two of Manco's brothers. Juan Pizarro was one of the few Spaniards to die in the fighting. Many Incas fled to where Manco had already retreated to Ollantaytambo outside of Cusco.

Manco then retreated to Vitcos. The Incas successfully repelled a Spanish attack on Manco at Vitcos and they were forced to retreat and regroup. From then on Manco was more or less on the run with his guards who continued to fend off the Spaniards at various points who never ceased to hunt down Manco. This included a ten-day battle at Vilcabamba which still stands as another of the cherished victories the Incas gained in order to keep Manco from Spanish forces. For a whole year Manco went on a victory march around the valley going from town to town occasionally having to repel Spanish attacks, including a ten-day battle with each side on opposite banks of a river, before settling back in Vilcabamba. During his travels he came to realize that the Guancas, a rival indigenous tribe were now fully allied with the Spaniards, and his guards were forced into battle with the Guancas.

The Inca defense was valiant, but the Spanish would prove an indefatigable force that constructed an ever more increasing amount of alliances with native factions who rivaled Manco's own forces. The dividing never ceased and after a couple years of running and fighting, Manco would inevitably drop his guard and succumb to the Spanish.

Spanish tactics only evolved with each failed capture of Manco. They would retreat from the methods of overt force and take a more nuanced approached.

Seven Spaniards (Almagristas, a group of Spaniards that broke away from Pizarro's leadership) whom he had given refuge approached Manco's camp at Vitcos, each on a different day, all proclaiming to be on the run for crimes committed, and protested to want to serve

Manco. After much suspicion they were finally accepted by the guards and Manco himself. For a couple years the men formed a brotherly relationship with Manco and his inner circle. It would prove to be a brutally pre-mediated plot to kill him. The men all decided that the time had come where Manco was vulnerable enough, and they stabbed the Inca ruler to death. The plot proved a bloody success, but the seven Spanish assassins were subsequently overrun and all killed by guards loyal to Manco in a most brutal manner.

His son, Sayri Tupac, was thought to have been poisoned by the Spanish and could be considered an even more naive and ineffective leader than his father by converting to Catholicism, the ultimate capitulation. He made a peace agreement but was ultimately worthless as Spanish conquest continued after his death.

The next Inca heir and ruler would be Manco's other son Titu Cusi, whose name awesomely translates to "The Magnanimous and The Fortunate," is almost single handedly responsible for the Inca account of much of the history of the first encounters with the Spaniards. There is no account from the Inca perspective other than that of Titu Cusi who told the story of the internal struggles and the turmoil created by the arrival of the Spanish. Without this account, next to nothing of the internal events of the Inca power structure remains and we would have to depend on less reliable Spanish sources. Titu Cusi's account of the conquest was explicit in its description of the conqueror's greed, violence and lusting actions.

Titu Cusi's reign would be short lived and his story came to a close when he succumbed to pneumonia and died. The last indigenous ruler in the blood line was Tupac Amaru. For those who care about bloodlines, and monarchists do, he was executed, and Inca rule had officially come to a close. The Spanish appetite for conquest never wavered and they continued to wreak havoc. At the death of Tupac Amaru the Spanish finally lost interest in having a favorable local leader to play puppet and no longer sought to be considered as visitors, they whole-heartedly took on the role as conquerors and were now the sole rulers of what would become known as Peru.

Power in Peru remained a ruthless endeavor and even with a firm grip on it the power struggle shifted to the Spaniards themselves. With the local challenge entirely subdued they started fighting amongst each other over gold won in battles and paid ransoms. Factions formed amongst the Spanish, mainly the Amalgrista's who broke away from the aging Pizarro, were the main challengers, led by Almagro who naturally, in such a climate was executed by one of Pizarro's brothers. Pizarro would ultimately prevail in that first civil strife but fighting continued and one of Almagro's sons would kill Pizarro. After proclaiming himself governor he was also killed by the new official governor selected by the King of Spain. In a sense nothing had changed in this land. Only the names and faces of the men who replaced one another through similarly violent means.

Power had gone to the heads of nearly all involved in this collision of empires. The Spanish became just as susceptible to the civil strife that quickly infected the Inca ruling class in the earliest days of conquest. Spanish control of Peru was steadfast until the 19th century when Peru struggled for its independence. In the early years of the struggle for power, brutality was ever present. There was almost a code, and violence was a way of life. This common way or this code of that time was explained no better than when Atahuallpa, the first Inca ruler who came into contact with Pizarro and the Spanish, said, "If you disrespect me, I will disrespect you."

****

It is hard to believe that something like the potato is not indigenous to Ireland. It indeed came from Peru. It is also true that the tomato made a similar journey from South America to Italy. It is a fact less difficult to believe when confronted with the grand agricultural terraces of the Sacred Valley. These concise structures and neatly shaped indentations into various hills and mountainsides dot the valley and remain both utilized and left to crumble, but nevertheless are relics to the ingenuity and thoughtfulness of the Incas.

I set out for Moray on the bus and got off at an intersection in the middle of a field beside which there was a small shack of a church with a toy size cross tacked onto the peak of the roof. A few taxis hovered nearby, and I found a ride with one. A man named Pedro drove me around for the next few hours. Along the way we dodged donkeys running in front of us and together we pushed the stubborn donkeys to the side of the road. When he stopped at home for lunch he brought me a Tupperware bowl of rice and chicken, and insisted we have lunch together.

I was strongly taken with the beauty of Moray. Its beautifully curved agricultural terraces looked more a work of land art rather than the testing ground for growing different kinds of crops that the Incas had once used it for. The large circular terraces were depressed deep into the ground, creating a great difference in temperature at each level.

It was an easy place to sit peacefully and enjoy the unique view for an hour or two. I sloppily drew the terraces out on a small piece of paper and assured myself I would build something similar one day on a smaller scale. Hundreds of questions arose in the mind, but I was none too bothered with getting any answers as the circular terraces were a pure work of beauty, and beauty is a sufficient answer. To the eye of a foreigner, most of the sites of the valley leave one with a deep feeling of wonder. I wondered how I was only coming to see and know about such a place at this late date. These stones had been moved to this spot hundreds of years earlier. For all the concerted effort I made to get to this distant spot, there somehow remained a feeling of randomness to this encounter. It was a place of work, but it also looked a place of worship, where beauty could be seen from every vantage point and every angle, yet it was undoubtedly a place where hardship was a near constant aspect of life. It was a place that appeared unbreakable, and difficult for all the people making the attempt to trek across its terraces, yet it was the work of humans. Everywhere one looked, there was the result of a massive human endeavor. There was no need for explanation, being present was enough, it was simply a wonderful place to be.

****

The same could be said for the other sites of the valley such as the glorious city of Pisac and the regal Ollantaytambo. The wind made everything a balancing act the further one climbed, but all were filled with a desire to reach the top or get across the various sites that were undoubtedly foreign to their eyes and the bottoms of their feet. Faithful tourists struggled to climb each of the ruined cities like religious pilgrims. Their religion being travel. A religion can be boiled down to routine actions. For the faithful traveler there is a steady routine in getting to places, experiencing them and making them into memories to return home with and pass on what one saw, and spreading a kind of nomadic gospel. Occasionally converting sedentary types into fellow nomads.

Pisac and Ollantaytambo are noble precursors to Machu Picchu. Nearly as impressive, both are built into large hillsides, yet so naturally integrated that they appear to have grown outwards from the earth. A few rooftops are covered as an example of how the rest of the structures were once enclosed and sheltered the Incas from the elements, but most are bare and more comfortable in a ruined state.

There is a distinct beauty to things that are half-gone. They have fallen and crumbled in places, in others there has been an obvious process of rebuilding. The houses and buildings become distinct from the land and in their ruined state resemble islands slowly washing away. There are frequent reminders of the Inca empire and in many ways it is visible and still lives on but no more so than in the stones of the Sacred Valley. There is no attempt to polish or hide the stones that form the basis of these cities and structures. The kingdom of the Incas is an earthly one. Each site thoroughly impressive not only because of their settings but because of the ingenuity and attention to detail paid throughout the cities.

I was excited to get on the train to Aguas Calientes, the little town sat below Machu Picchu. There was not a frown to be seen on the train and the weather matched everyone's pleasant expressions. At the end of the train line was an entirely different climate. I had watched the landscape become greener the further we went, but only felt its humidity and wetness when the doors of the train opened. Immediately there were hundreds of tourists and thousands of things being sold, but the most prevalent sound was that of the Urubamba river rushing alongside the bottom of the mountain on which Machu Picchu is set. I felt as though I had arrived in a natural waterpark. The atmosphere remained cheery as I settled into the humid little town, until I found a seat in the small square when one of the saddest things happened.

I heard a woman say with trembling shock in her voice that Robin Williams had died. I will never forget the sound of her voice. It was as though she was talking about a child of her own. It sounded silly for a moment to feel distraught over the death of a celebrity, but the shock everyone around suddenly began to feel and show on their faces was palpable and revealed just what a happy force he was. There was a joy that was suddenly taken from everyone. Everyone immediately realized what his death meant, that the world was bound to be less funny and would never be as funny as it once was.

The death of Robin Williams lingered. For it was evident he was not merely a comedian but someone whose death could feel like the world lost a king. Most every conversation was consumed with the disbelief that someone so funny who could make light of anyone and anything was no longer alive. It was perhaps the least funny day that there has ever been. Even rewatching clips of his television appearances and shows proved fruitless for it was impossible to remove oneself from the grief of him suddenly being gone. We were not in San Francisco or New York or London. The sadness of his passing traveled to the edge of the Amazon and left a mark. We were at the edge of a jungle in South America and the sorrow of his death would remain long after we had left.

Half of those sleeping in Aguas Calientes think they are going to get up early enough to be the first into Machu Picchu. It is dark when they reach the line for the bus which stretches a hundred people back and after I got in the line another hundred quickly fall in behind.

Aguas Calientes is a peculiar little amalgamation. A town that merely exists as a jumping off point, it takes on the character of an outdoor theater lobby. Everyone is a guest here for the same show. The only difference is that some will go to the top of Machu Picchu in a bus or climb the steep path on foot. People from all over the world but mostly Europe and America are funneled into this little holding pen to eat Peruvian Pizzas and buy tchotchkes before looking at one of the most beautiful and mystical set of ruins in the world.

No matter how manicured and beautifully set the Inca retreat is, it still is a city in ruins. Even in its incomplete state a foreigner is naturally deceived by the inherent beauty of its setting and shape and concludes that it's missing pieces only slightly detract from its beauty that otherwise appears resoundingly complete.

The visitors are not pushy or mean, but rather eager and energetic, everyone naturally exudes some kind of civil patience as to not spoil the beauty and tranquility of the sight. Some have even brought their dog in a backpack. Everyone is resoundingly happy for they are just below a place they have dreamed about and have a bubbling anticipation to see. Everyone is happy, there are few places, perhaps none, where the crowds of people create a collective and infectious smile without being told to do so. There are no little town scams going on near Machu Picchu. The days of ripping off tourists on arrival are gone, if anything they pay too much before they leave home. It is far too lucrative a site for the atmosphere to be spoiled with pushy guides and con artists. Well-armed and armored police provide more than a touch of authority and make sure of this.

The magnificence of Machu Picchu makes everyone feel as though it is a unique and exclusive experience because no matter how many people come through this distant patch at the edge of the continent's vast rain forest it always remains a fresh sight. The journey is too long and requires at least some sort of calculation on the part of even the most well off of travelers to consider it cliché.

The cloud of mystery hovers over no less of Machu Picchu than the rest of the culture that gave birth to it. It has been somewhat agreed upon due to various factors that the site was likely a seasonal place of pleasure for the Inca elite. Where all sorts of debauched activities took place including the sacrifice of young girls. Just like Juanita the Ice Maiden the remains of young girls have been found at Machu Picchu. It was a retreat for Inca rulers where along with other extracurriculars such sacrifices were likely common place.

In the time that one lingers around Aguas Calientes there is little to do and one day in a restaurant overlooking the river I noticed two Peruvians sitting on rocks in the river with hammers monotonously pounding away at some stones. There seemed little reason for this almost ancient activity. The rocks they broke up were not even sorted or collected and carried away. They were simply thrown back into the river for what I could only assume was a way to smooth out and shrink the rocks in order make the river flow more quickly. It was a hopeful thought, but it also looked like a kind of punishment. The dullness alone was punishment in itself but after a few hours it would take the shape of a physical punishment.

Behind them was the lush vine covered hill that rises up to Machu Picchu, a constant reminder of its wild location, and none of the modern developments of Aguas Calientes could be seen. The green is so dense, it makes Machu Picchu seem all the more hidden, and unbelievable.

The two men hammering was indicative of the arduous human exertion required to create such a place as Machu Picchu. After looking at these two men, I thought differently not only of Machu Picchu but of all the ruins I had seen in the Sacred Valley.

The Inca kingdom is dead and gone, but their language survives, the people have the same faces they always had in these mountains and more than anything the work ethic of the people of the Sacred Valley remains vivid in every cultivated patch of land or wherever there may be a structured piling of stones. The more Inca sites I walked amongst and the more people I met and saw using ancient methods of cultivation the more I could see that empire in the flesh.

The first few buses all looked for a single person to fill an empty seat, so I got to the top before the sun rose over the mountain. My first glimpse was similar to how it must appear at night. Its stones glow in the dark like flesh. The whole of the city becomes one large nocturnal tree at rest; still, yet living. It was not the top of a mountain, but the top of a tree. For a mountain top is possible to reach, but a tree is impossible to rest atop, and only birds are privileged enough to experience. But here we all were at an impossible place. As beautiful as nature is, it is man that did this. It is a city that floats, a city above all others and all things even the surrounding mountains that are visibly higher, Machu Picchu is somehow above those, too.

Machu Picchu is fine art - one of the world's highest creations - the artists who created it were likely slaves, and we will never know their names. But we know their creation, and in acknowledging it they have our empathy and certainly our admiration. The few thousand people climbing around Machu Picchu make it difficult to consider the site dead or ruined.

The more I read about the human nature of the dying Inca empire the more real the characters resembled those of revolutions and wars of the most told stories of Europe and Asia. To delve deeply into the history of the Incas, to walk in their footsteps and touch the stones that they painfully hammered, carried and stacked is to be as close to them as one can. The connection with the past is possible and equally palpable, for they are not merely a part of the tragedy that is Spanish conquest but a living being whose life was long and grand for hundreds of years before the arrival of the armies of distant kings. The stories of each Inca ruler carry a tragic and peculiar demise, so much so that the circumstances in which they were deposed and killed make the worrying expressions on their faces easily imagined.

The third day I went to Macchu Picchu I found the most secluded spot on one of the terraces that draped downwards off the side of the mountain. I thought of how the Spanish never found Machu Picchu, it was a secret successfully kept. Machu Picchu never disappeared it was merely hidden, there was no map for it to exist on, its whereabouts, existed like much of Inca history, in the minds of the Incas. It was only lost to those who had never seen it. That's why Machu Picchu had been considered a lost city until 1911 do to the relentlessness of the jungle. American traveler Hiram Bingham made the modern discovery of it. But locals who had always known of its presence, showed him the way.

Gustave Flaubert, in his journey through the Middle East noted that the stones at Baalbek were in deep thought. I found the stones of the Sacred Valley to not just be in deep thought but to be living. Any stone that is given such care and thought is injected with a kind of life, a mind, and still lives even when it lay in ruins. Perhaps its life is born before that, when it is chiseled from the quarry or the mountainside. Therein lies the sanctity of this land the Incas consider sacred, because they gave it something of themselves and made it so, not only in thought but in action do they make it sacred.

As I lounged on the lowest terrace resting my head on a stone I looked at the surrounding mountains covered with vines that grow at a relentless pace no matter how often they are cut back. It was an awe-inspiring sight to look out at from this most perfect setting. I then thought of how the stones placed in this spot more than five hundred years earlier were just as indefatigable.

The Inca empire, its kings and its laborers are long gone, but I was certain that they never died for they remain where they have always been. They live in the stones of the Sacred Valley.

17

Lima

After a couple weeks in the mountains and endless stretches of land that surround Cusco, I was somewhat dazed to be looking at the Pacific Ocean once again as I rode in a taxi on the coastal road towards the heart of Lima. No longer did I have to feel the effects of altitude, nor was I chewing coca leaves to relieve those annoying effects. The cliffs that line one side of the road made me feel as though I was riding on the Pacific Coast Highway below Santa Monica. I had been on much of that highway before and this road felt like a continuation of it. There was a connection between the entirety of the Pacific coastline that stretches the length of both American continents. A twenty-minute taxi ride made this clear to me.

Being near an ocean provided the same healthy feeling it always does. There would be no more difficult mountain conditions, tirelessly walking up and down hills or steps and steeply rising streets, using more energy than is needed, and becoming tired more quickly. I was relieved to no longer see the Quechuan women labor up those steep streets in Cusco with sacs of cloth or vegetables on their backs or endlessly sewing hats and sweaters, while selling them more or less at the same time on the street. The people in the Sacred Valley were strong and durable. Their lives and characters were built on physical labor, and even though they looked strong and more than capable of handling any physical task put in front of them, they looked tired. It is a grueling life to grow crops, cultivate land and all the things that come with a life of subsistence living. They were so close to the earth it was as if they grew out of it just like the crops they cultivated. The sun was intense and life up there was perhaps more simple being closer to the earth and stars. There were beautiful landscapes, a rich culture and history, but no matter how simple or quiet it was, it was stressful to me. It is a life of strenuous physical work. The people of the Sacred Valley were so salt of the earth it is as though the earth was caked into their skin and teeth. Their hands almost completely calloused. I was happy to be in a city, more so in one near an ocean.

The immensity of Lima could be felt while swiftly traveling alongside it. There was a similarity to the city of Los Angeles, as they both start or end, depending on your viewpoint, at the ocean and sprawl inland. Unlike Los Angeles it was conquered and settled from the ocean. Though the settlement of the city started from its coastline and goes from west to east. I thought that this was why it was a little less tied to the land mass it is attached to. It sits perched on an edge, like a large villa on the Amalfi coast. Also, like Los Angeles it endlessly consumes more land with each passing year.

It was quickly evident there were many sides to the city, and it would prove difficult to see all of them without settling down for a year. The kind of place where walking between neighborhoods takes an hour and no one bothers to do so. Los Angeles has its flare ups of smog, but in Lima there was not a spec of blue in the sky, because for nearly half the year it is covered by a complete white fog, that is simply or rather playfully known as the blanket.

I was in two minds of what to do in such an enormous place. It was a new city, one I had never seen before, but I was at the end of my journey and having spent the last few weeks trekking up and down the steep Inca ruins of the Sacred Valley I was tired and did not have much desire for museums, ticking off a list of sites or making the long treks between neighborhoods. I knew there was a sea of life in Lima to be seen and had, but instead, I swiftly made my way to the pleasant Miraflores neighborhood and to the counter of an old school eatery called Manolo's. A happy place where there were sandwiches piled high in display cases. Along the way I bought a large cigar and tucked it into my coat pocket and decided to smoke it after a long lunch. The menacing side of Lima was nowhere to be found. The waiters in bow-tie moved at great speed to serve people who ate and drank at a snail's pace. I sat at the little counter eating Churritos covered in chocolate syrup, then dipped them in Cortados, whilst chatting to the old ladies who came to the bar alone to do the same as part of a daily routine. All were either widows or older single women. No one took off their jacket even though they stayed awhile, me included. The air was cool, but our coats stayed on us like blankets. Even though it was my first time there, it felt familiar and easy to sink in to. We all had the smiles of satisfied children when we looked at each other, and when looking straight ahead our faces went back to a state of complete relaxation and were pleased to watch the afternoon slowly glide by. I was happy to be in a city, by the ocean, and not at a high altitude with an oppressive sun. I belonged in a city or at least close to one. The more I sat and watched food being brought out by well-dressed men, I further realized how stuck in time the people up in the Sacred Valley were. They were still centuries behind, even if they enjoyed it, that's where they were. Everything about Lima was modern. It was now easy to see the harsh realities of both worlds and the accompanying lifestyles. But cities, are places of convenience, not necessarily for all, but everything one needs is never far, it's just a matter of getting it. Everything is there, it just takes a few dollars or some persuasive words. Rural life means being distant from everything, which can be pleasurable at times, but it mostly means spending much of your time waiting for something or someone to get there and fix a situation or fill a need.

The neighborhood also quickly felt like home and for a few days I rarely left the area surrounding the urban park in the middle of Miraflores. I went back to the cigar shop and bought a bunch of Cubans to make the afternoons feel even more lazy. Other than a few slow and short walks I spent much of my time in the park talking to whomever sat next to me. More than a couple of overly friendly drug dealers, including the same one three nights in row. Each night he pretended as if he did not remember me, until I called him out on it. I tried talking to him about himself, to figure him out, but he had little to say, he was busy trying to sell drugs to tourists and looked anxious at the lack of prospects or perhaps the consequences of not selling enough. He was mean looking, and I wondered if he had always been that way. A twenty-six-year-old mad-faced Colombian from Medellín wearing a camouflage jacket, riding his bike tried to befriend me by borrowing my lighter. All he had to say about Medellín was how crazy it was, and a few minutes later bluntly tried to sell me cocaine. When I said I was not interested in drugs he adjusted the gears on his bike and pedaled down the sidewalk. I could not help but be amused by the presence of so many drug dealers on bikes. I also spoke with some of the musicians and painters taking a break from selling or making their art.

A nerdy young girl of seventeen came up to me looking to practice her English and she had spiky teeth that had not completely grown in. Her English was not very good, and she talked of wanting to study at Cambridge or Oxford, naturally. She had a thick accent, but not one that was solely based in Spanish. The way she pronounced some English words sounded as if she had been a native speaker of Japanese. When I asked her where her parents were from, I was not surprised.

"My father is from Peru, but he is Japanese. My mother is

Peruana." I encouraged and assisted her attempts at English as much as I could before she was on her way. I remained intrigued by her being of partially Japanese descent, yet still native to Peru. The Japanese community in Peru is significant. In fact, there are a lot of Japanese in Lima and there was none more infamous than its recently imprisoned former President Alberto Fujimori who ruled in office for the whole of the 1990's. Miraflores was a neighborhood with many Japanese people and was the birthplace and childhood home of Fujimori. Fujimori had peacefully come to power by easily beating the writer, future Nobel prize winner, and politically centrist Mario Vargas Llosa. Llosa was surprisingly, even to himself, popular throughout the election but lost by twenty percentage points in the final vote. Llosa seems like one of the few sane if not unrealistically logical politicians to get that far in Peruvian politics. It is no surprise that Llosa had quite a lot to say, after the defeat about the doings of his opponent, notably labeling them 'rats.' Llosa has clashed since the sixties with other Latin American writers on politics, being one of the earliest critics of Castro's regime in Cuba and other dictators who popped up over the years in the region. He famously got into it with another famed writer, Gabriel Garcia Marquez (Gabo), and Gabo was seen shortly after a meeting between the two with a black eye. Llosa on politics is, if not unreasonably hopeful, his arguments are clear and concise when describing the political diseases that not only Latin American countries face but politics in general, "dictatorship is the manifestation of...everything evil." Thus, there was no man in a better position or more well equipped to understand what Fujimori's victory meant for the people of Peru.

The peace ended with Fujimori's election and his regime systematically looted the country's treasury handing out millions in bribes and favors and kept a grip on power by torturing and killing political opponents. Fujimori was not the only ruthless man in power at the time and benefited a great deal from having some equally if not more ruthless enforcers positioned throughout his regime. None more notorious than the head of Peruvian Intelligence, was the sensationally named Vladimiro Montesinos, his full name being, Vladimiro Lenin Ilich Montesinos Torres. A ruthless man who ultimately played a part in the conviction of his former boss as well as many other high ranking Peruvian officials, some low ranking ones too, as a result of his video-recording many of the meetings between himself and politicians, businessmen, executives, and all other walks of life of Peruvian society that came to him for protection and favors and nasty jobs. Torture of political prisoners and opponents and anyone who got in the way was also recorded. It is said that over ten thousand hours of tapes were recorded during Montesinos career, yet only some have been made entirely public.

Fujimori was more or less in the clear at the end of his reign, but it made sense to flee to Japan where he holds dual citizenship, in order to avoid the tentacles of his predecessor. In 2005 he made the mistake of thinking he could travel to the South American continent and escape the net of Peruvian justice system that was now on a more straight and narrow course, five years after his ouster and seeking to punish him for his crimes. Having flown to Santiago, Chile on a private jet from Tokyo via Tijuana, the plane had accidentally crossed into Peruvian airspace, thus giving the Peruvians jurisdiction over the flight landing in Chile. He was swiftly arrested in Santiago and brought to Peru to trial to face dozens of corruption charges. His cooperation and repayment of nearly seventy-five million dollars led to a swift trial which he did not have to testify in, which would likely have led to more charges and scandals but did nothing to shorten his sentence which in Peru the maximum one can receive is twenty-five years.

One of the charges Fujimori faced had to do with a long standing battle he had with the Maoist separatists group Shining Path, who had committed a number of violent acts itself including raiding the residence of the Japanese ambassador and taking hostage more than a hundred guests including Fujimori's mother and brother, and future president of Peru Alejandro Toledo. But Fujimori's response was indicative of his heavy hand which resulted in more charges from the new administration. Fujimori called in special forces, and the standoff was soon ended with one hostage dead, and a controversy ensued over the deaths of all the hostage takers most likely by being summarily executed. Vladimiro Montesinos was complicit and used the very same tactics in conjunction with Fujimori to combat insurgents along with pursuing his personal political and financial agenda. This was not the first time that Fujimori or Montesinos had been ruthless in dealing with this revolutionary group and death squads became a regular tactic in Fujimori's government. The arrest of the two men led to Montesinos revelation of the tapes and he was dealt with somewhat more leniently than the former president who is serving a minimum prison term of twenty years in Peru.

****

Outside of the Governmental Palace was a scattering of riot police and military officers preparing for a ceremony of some sorts. The sky was more grey than it had been the past week and it was not even noon. I expected it to rain, but there was none on its way, just humidity. It was like an unusually warm winter's day. Tourists and locals alike watched curiously, waiting to see the simple acts of pomp and circumstance performed by a few politicians or perhaps they enjoyed watching the workers set up the bleachers and a small stage. The sounds of hammers, power tools and wood being unloaded from a truck were constant and one man barking orders at the rest, and at times slapping his hands together instead of having to shout. I grew tired of waiting to see another politician wave for a few brief moments and decided to wander.

I left and went to Barrio Chino to get lost and see something a little more stimulating than politicians. The city's Chinatown was an overly dirty place, every building had grime on the side of it with several pungent odors rising from puddles collected alongside the curbs of streets and nearly every pothole or crack in the road. The streets had not been cleaned for some time. There were rows of restaurants down a pedestrian street the same colors of the Forbidden City. Every Chinese restaurant one has ever seen is recreated on this little street in Lima's Barrio Chino. Ducks hanging in a window, men taking large meat cleavers to the necks of those ducks and chickens, the walls simply decorated and waiters who take your order in a more than forthright manner. Even the hostesses holding menus outside the restaurants are dressed the same as the ones in New York or London.

No matter how nice a Chinese restaurant may be, it always feels like a soup-kitchen. Everyone slurping on spoons or grabbing meat with sticks makes for a perfectly plebeian meal accompanied by the usual bodily sounds any visitor to China knows full well. Just like any other exile community, Chinese expatriate communities hardly ever fully integrate into the country they have settled. It is peculiar how Chinese culture exists in nearly every country, mainly because of how little it differs from place to place as well as how rarely it fully integrates into each country. This is certainly the case in the western hemisphere and even in Europe. In western countries, exile communities have more freedom to stay the same, or less pressure to change than in say, an African country or the Middle East where there is a long-established culture in some way pushing them back from or into that community.

Arriving into a Chinatown is always sudden, because of the bluntness of Chinese culture and it is an assault on the senses. It is a culture easily recognized and unnoticeably different from any other. As suddenly as one arrives in a Chinatown it is an equally quick escape from the country you are in. There is also something constant about each one. One knows what they are getting in a Chinatown, the guarantee of being a foreigner, even in one's own country, more or less the same way you would be in China. A foreigner in a Chinatown always knows their place, which is being politely ignored and interactions with people tend towards the commercial sort. Everything is about money and everything is for sale. No one, at least no Chinese person is idle or idling, and those that do stand still, look foolish or helpless.

Not that I was expecting to, but it is very difficult to feel like one is a part of Chinese culture. With travel, there is always an element of trying to immerse oneself or walk in the shoes of other cultures. It is nearly impossible to do so in Chinese culture, not merely because of the difficulties of learning its language or its differences in customs, but because being a part of Chinese culture for the most part is centered around being racially Chinese. Chinese culture is far from porous and in fact is tightly sealed. This is not hard to make out from the lack of diversity in China itself and its bubble like living wherever its culture may be around the world.

To the Chinese, China is the center of the world, and in one way or another it has always been an empire. But empires are more subtle these days. Chinese communities grow more so than say Japanese communities in places like San Francisco or São Páolo, which are well established communities and neighborhoods. But Chinatowns are always a more significant presence and nearly always permanent and certainly more defined. There is no mistaking where one is when passing through a Chinatown. In the Liberdade neighborhood of São Páolo, one can easily forget they are in a Japanese neighborhood, or even in San Francisco's Little Tokyo. Neither of these take hold and dominate the neighborhoods they settle in quite like Chinese culture. The same goes for more than a few large Indian communities in places like South Africa, Kenya, Uganda, and Trinidad. Each neighborhood has left its impact on the city but not like even the most simple of Chinatowns. China has steadily and at times rapidly grown over the past half century into an empire built on commerce and its race, and in this little section of Lima, was a piece of it.

Just beyond the long pedestrian street lined with Chinese restaurants there was a large covered market selling mostly meat and fish. The smell of raw meat in a warm place naturally gave the place an air of death and agitated the gag reflex. Overfed flies flew from carcass to carcass and some hovered in slow circles around piles of meat waiting to be sold. Meat sellers yelled frantically at employees and one another about simple tasks. Blood was mixed with soap in streaks across the floor as a result of mediocre attempts to keep the place clean. The floor was completely wet in most places and walking through the market was similar to navigating rocks in a river. I walked carefully, at times nervously because of the thought of falling into such a mess. The sights and smells of Chinatown were tiring, just like being in China. The grime of the street was on everyone's face.

The thing that is always superficially fascinating about every Chinatown, is the fact that there are so many Chinese people in such a seemingly random place. Always oddly isolated and homogenized. Whether it be in Havana or in Milan, it has a peculiar way of making one not feel so out of place or foreign. And when you leave Chinatown, it is suddenly gone, having little to do with any other part of the city. When you leave, you almost forget it is there.

There were a number of narrow pedestrian side streets that jutted out to and from the market and were not a part of Barrio Chino. These streets had no Chinese stores or even Chinese people and were only peopled by Peruvians. I was suddenly back in Lima, back in Peru, and back in South America. It was momentarily surreal and felt as though I had been swiftly moving between continents. Each street filled with people shopping and selling parts for one machine or another. I wandered around and found most of them lined with small food stalls each manned either by a single woman or an entire family. As I walked, I began to look closely at the faces of the street vendors. They looked decidedly different from most people I had seen in Peru. Everyone on these small pedestrian streets was poor. There was no doubting that. The faces of people did not merely give the image of poverty, but of a kind that was particularly hard up. There is worse poverty to be seen and even worse in Peru and Lima for that matter, but I could not help but notice a particularly grim nature to their expressions. The constant murky grayness of the sky was no help, lasting all day and contributing to the glib setting. Everyone's face was made a little more solemn by it. It is commonly said of those who have little that they do not know what they are missing or are content with what they have. But here on these small sides streets there was no ignorance. These poor faces were tired and worn out. There was no sense of ignorance being bliss. Nothing was bliss. They were well aware of what they did not have and were none too pleased about it. Even though it was poor, it was not menacing. There was no one openly selling drugs and the streets were not laced with its residual effects, nor was there a turf war being fought. These were the good people of Lima who were suffering from the effects of making an honest living. Everyone was well to do even if they were none too pleased about it.

Most of them sold the same things, making the fate of each stall seem even more dire, because of so much competition nearby. Each stall had a large steel salad bowl filled with white and yellow colored ceviche, besides a pile of the wonderfully named Churrasco Choclo, which was more or less strips of fried pork, mostly fat, and another big bowl of oversized steamed corn. A few others had large steel bowls filled with gelato and small pitchers of chocolate fudge sauces waiting to be poured on. Some selling cigarettes out of a boxy tray that hung from a strap around their neck like a cocktail waitress at a casino.

When I indicated I wanted one, each member of the family took on a task within the little counter space of the cart. One ladled the ceviche while another picked pieces of Churrasco with tongs, and another folded a napkin around a plastic fork and knife. And another scooped out some steamed corn with a pink measuring cup. I sat on a small plastic stool more or less in the middle of a crowd expecting it to break. Hundreds of people quickly walking past nearly brushed into me and angling around like a pack of motorbikes. They then gave me a cup of pomegranate juice in a flimsy plastic cup and I had all I needed. Apart from it being some of the best ceviche I ever had, it cost three dollars. I wondered about the journey the fish had taken from the ocean to this bowl of ceviche to my plate. How long ago had it been caught? The trucks it had been on, how long it had been in the bowl of citrus and milk? Where did they get their food that they sold? Did they catch it themselves? Eating a fulfilling meal such as this one, for three dollars which would easily be thirty in New York made my head swim with thoughts of the lopsidedness of the world. It suddenly flipped the world on its head. Nothing made sense. The poor always cook well, therefore in a sense they eat well. There is always good food in the poorest places. Afterwards I was full and satisfied. I did not eat lunch in Barrio Chino, because everything looked like it would hurt my stomach and I almost expected the same from these carts on the street. But everything was fresh and satisfying, making me feel like I was in someone's home.

I wandered my way back to the Plaza Mayor and was curious to see if the tourists and locals were still waiting for the ceremony. To my surprise it had all come and gone and the bleachers were being disassembled. The politician had done what he needed to do and as expected everything was the same. Even the soldiers were done for the day and whipped the sides of their horses to begin trotting down the cobble stone streets that zigzagged towards Barrio Chino.

Each soldier was overdressed in a ceremonial uniform, which looked as though they were crusaders storming the Holy Land. The soldiers trotted in silver Romanesque helmets with red bristles jutting out the top. They wore red pants, high black boots, beneath black coats with red stripes down the arms and large silver buttons in front. The horses' manes were braided with red and yellow thread and were confidently shitting while running...or running while shitting... forming a line of shit for half a mile that turned with the narrow streets. Each soldier held a ceremonial spear in one hand and one soldier managed to somehow stay on his horse without holding the reigns as his other hand held a Blackberry to his ear.

At the edge of the square were policemen unceremoniously dressed in black fatigues looking like mercenaries, which perhaps was the perfect camouflage for patrolling a city at night. The butts of the pistols and larger guns they carried were banged up and looked like they had not only been used to shoot with but to hit people. The shotguns held upwards and resting against a shoulder with one hand carried the color of un-polished steel, but somehow glistened under the grayness of the clouds. Each man wore large mirrored aviator glasses and while looking at them the whole of the plaza could be seen as if through a fish eye lens.

Only a part of their faces was exposed along with their thick hands that looked like the ends of baseball bats. The glasses were so much a part of the look of these men that they likely wore them to bed and in the ocean and the shower, and of course while having sex. They were menacing men without eyes made more menacing by the mysterious stone faces they had underneath those glasses. They were the faces of men ready for a long gunfight and indeed men who knew how to fight and kill. They were a sight unto themselves. Servicemen tend to carry a heroic quality, but theirs were strictly authoritative. After the ceremonial soldiers and the politicians had gone along with the tourists and other bystanders, the lessening of light in the sky meant that the neighborhood would soon put on its more forbidding face. And as I walked back to my room, I realized only the eyeless men were brave enough to remain.

****

My days in Lima were restful, satisfying, happy, revitalizing, and filled with many pleasant conversations with locals. For the most part I stayed in Miraflores and Barranco. When I did venture out it was not far, just to sit on the cliffs and watch the surfers waiting patiently in the water for the perfect wave. Along the sidewalks atop the cliffs were beautiful women, possibly trophy wives working out, equipped with oversized boob jobs and some even sported fresh bandages over their noses.

As big as Lima was, it began to feel like a small outpost. I looked downwards from the cliffs and even though I recognized how large they were, they were dwarfed by the distance of the horizon and the coastline that took miles to disappear. No matter how big South American cities become, they are minuscule compared to the mass of the continent, and those on the coast, by the ocean they sit next to. There was no such thing as a crowded country. As quickly as the population of the continent grows, it barely makes its mark.

I wondered how much more could I travel. The constant motion was making me tired and at times less aware of the town or city I was in. I was eager to sit on the beach in Colombia for a few days, and a part of me was eager to get home. A month in Peru felt like a long time. Some of the people I met had traveled in Peru for three months, from one end to the other. That seemed like an eternity. Though I was eager to be on my way, I felt dissatisfied that I had only seen the nicer parts of Lima. I did not want to leave having only seen its pleasant side.

I knew there were violent sections of Lima, but you rarely see the violence because it is more or less segregated to certain neighborhoods or barrios and takes place in the dark. I came to find out that when asking directions, people would explain how to get somewhere by what to avoid. Almost every day I ate ceviche, and was fascinated by how good it was, but also by how many creative and diverse versions there are of it and I had heard of a few good ceviche restaurants in very bad neighborhoods, where all the best food always is. When I asked for directions from a few people, they all gave the same answer. It is the best place for ceviche in all of Peru, but you must take a taxi as it is not safe to walk, and you must have a car waiting outside for you. With a number of other places I asked directions to, I got similar answers, "Do not go here at night. Avoid this barrio night and day, you cannot walk, you must be in a car." "Do not try to walk to or from there." Everyone was well aware of what was bad, and there was little reason, perhaps besides ceviche to go to such neighborhoods. Danger was never far in Lima. A few told me not to go at all.

I left Miraflores and the other more pleasant neighborhoods of Lima for Centro and Barrio Chino, not the worst neighborhoods Lima had to offer, but they had a decidedly more aggressive and desperate face than Miraflores. It was a long drive on a highway that went through the center of the city. I had the idea that Miraflores was the center of the city, but Centro in the north was technically the center. The cab driver talked the entire ride about how he wanted to move to France, with interjections on being careful in Centro. "Be in your hotel before dark." He was another Peruvian looking to go abroad to escape the things that happen in the dark.

****

The next day I walked further into obscure and desolate neighborhoods at the edges of Centro. I even went back to Barrio Chino eager to take in more of the copious sights and smells. I enjoyed the grittiness of it. It was even livelier on this day. Eventually I found myself back in Plaza Mayor late in the afternoon and again I suddenly became tired and nearly exhausted. The hours I spent all morning on my feet quickly caught up with me. Whenever my body was a little bit rested, I was off wandering down the endless streets to see what life was like on them. I kept telling myself to rest, even though I was far too restless to do so. I could only take it easy when my legs shook with weakness from so much walking. The arches of my feet ached, and my knee bones were grinding together. My mind and body were having an argument and I was stuck in the middle of it. I found relief in a nearby cafe and enjoyed a nice meal, ordered coffee after coffee and espresso to at least perk my mind up.

Afterwards, I sat up against a building on the edge of the Plaza Mayor and watched some street performers jump about entertaining a small gathering of people. It was fun and I was beginning to feel relaxed. Much of my body was not just at rest, but nearly asleep from the petty stimulants of coffee and tobacco as well as from overindulging at the cafe.

I wanted to be on the beach in Colombia, with the promise of everything that Colombia promises. The beautiful women, the partying and the beaches. Everyone had bad things to say about Colombia too, of how dangerous it was, and this place to stay away from or that, and how to protect yourself. The list went on. I did not really care much about that, I wanted to take flight from this city that was getting grayer by the minute.

I had planned on flying to Colombia the next day and wanted

nothing to stop me from getting there. The thought of traversing more land on an overnight bus or walking through the Centro of Lima made me pine for a comfortable and quiet bed. I felt that spending a few days off my feet as I had done along the way, would no longer do the trick. But still all I could do was sit and relax, hoping to rejuvenate myself for the flight the next day.

The sound of the square was congenial and there were no panhandlers nor menacing faces; they stayed in the narrower and darker streets. The openness of the main square had a softening effect, just well to do people, a sprinkling of tourists, and others waiting to go back to shuffling papers. There was no need to talk to anyone as the stimulants were providing me a satisfying inner solitude. My worries fell away. I did not want to look for any more dangerous alleyways and I resigned myself to knowing that sometimes the best thing to do in a city is watch it happen and not take part. I was happy to be the flâneur of Lima for as long as the stimulants lasted in my body. I wanted to be anonymous and benefit as much as I could from being alone before returning home. I came to think I was invisible, and no one could see me. If you spend enough time alone, you occasionally forget that people can actually see you.

The street performers did the usual tricks and jokes that provided smiles. Though, the people watching was more interesting. I soon came to realize I was not invisible and at one point I noticed a young man watching the same street performers was occasionally watching me, too. I saw him in my peripheral and every time my head moved slightly his way, he made a point to get my attention without making it look like he was trying very hard. I was put off by him, but not by some sort of predatory feeling. From his gazes I could tell that he had a million questions for me and I was hardly in a state for being interviewed. I was a foreigner and could now feel myself sticking out, and thus a well of information and amusement as foreigners often are to locals. During the few days I wandered around Centro I had been wondering whether or not that would mean something in this unforgiving neighborhood or where it might lead to. He made it clear that I was not invisible. Some people love foreigners, because there is indeed always something new to hear from them.

With each look I made my best effort to seem disinterested and unapproachable, at times I closed my eyes as if to appear taking a nap whilst sitting on the curb. It did not work. His name was Italo and he dressed like a young comrade selling a political newspaper nobody wanted. Though, I would come to find out that he was actually a lawyer. He had a thin goatee and light brown skin that had not seen sun since the arrival of the blanket, and so pale it almost blended with the overcast sky beneath his jet-black hair. His tall frame looked odd sitting on the curb, his knees angling upwards, and he only did so in order to start a conversation. He politely began minding my business with some dull questions in the difficult way any conversation with a stranger begins. Making much of the label of my cigar, I gave it to him hoping, naively, he would be satisfied, but there was likely no gift or souvenir that would halt him from fulfilling his curiosity. I was rude, perhaps a side effect of too much Cuban tobacco, but he was determined to ask me questions and I gradually gave way. The only way out was to be curt, and that was something I had little reason to be at this point. Had I done so, I knew afterwards I would likely feel worse than him, besides, I suddenly felt like talking.

When I told him where I was from he had the same reaction to New York that everyone does. A place they indirectly know very well. "New York is so interesting; I see it all the time in movies and television." Italo said. My mind had been preoccupied with each city I was in and had not thought much about New York and suddenly I remembered how interesting New York was, too. Even the garbage you see on the street is interesting.

Italo talked about trivial things at first, but it was strangely all leading to one thing, a conversation about race. He wanted to know my history and ethnicity. Why I looked like I do. We discussed about where each of us was from then moved on to the diversity of Peru. He was a mestizo and like his parents had grown up in Lima. "People in Cusco are different than Lima, much more mestizo here, mixed European-Indian-African. Cusco and that part of the country is something all to itself, something different than us." Every country has its divisions and appear trivial to outsiders at first, simply because of their foreignness, but hearing Italo put it in terms of 'us' and 'them,' the divisions and differences of Peru were made vivid.

At the first mention of facial features, in reference to the differing appearances of Peruvians in Lima and those in and around Cusco, I began preparing myself for a diatribe. With an an unsatisfied look, he said, "everyone in Peru has black hair." Hoping to cheer him up, I said, "But look how full it always is. I have not seen a bald man yet, or a woman of any age with short hair. The girls always have hair down to the small of their back. So what's wrong with that?" I thought the mentioning of full hair would make him happy, because of how unhappy some become when the hair starts to thin and fade away.

"There is nothing interesting. No, how you say, "Vahr-ee-tee""

"Variety?"

"Yes, vahr-ee-tee. There is nothing like that."

He casually pointed side-ways with his pinky at my beard to make something of the color of the hair on my chin, an orangish red, and the blonde hair on my head. It was vivid to him, he said, as he wiped the back of his hand through his own beard. "I never seen this. Peru is just like China. Everyone has black hair."

When he said China, I could see the similarity in how hard working both cultures were, but he did not care much for that point. For some reason China, always became an ever more growing presence.

"There are different parts of China, where people look different than you might think. Do you know about this part of China called Xinjiang. They look different than the rest. Where the people are not Chinese. They are Uyghurs."

"India, too. All look like." Seemingly not paying attention to what I was saying.

"That's not true. I've seen Indians with red hair and red beards. India is a very diverse place. It is more than one country, really. There are many kinds of people."

It was odd to hear someone venting about the lack of diversity of one's country. It's usually the other way around. But better than hearing someone complaining about diversity.

With the beginning of any racial conversation, there is naturally, an unease of what path one will soon find themselves upon. Often there is little hope for anything positive, and it quickly descends into a lecture on the habits of certain groups: breeding habits, the smells of cooking, music etc. Though, quickly I realized Italo was uninterested in relating race to such things or anything negative for that matter. As he talked of different regions and countries around the world his face became layered with fascination when describing, say, the facial features of Uzbeks or Mongolians. It was not simply a discussion of race but one of history and how people came to be what and where they are. I knew how he felt. The same things were interesting to me.

His mind was in Asia, Central Asia, more specifically. Italo then took a napkin out of his pocket, delicately unfolded it and proceeded to draw a perfect map of Central Asia and parts of China and India as well. For some reason I was none too surprised by his ability to do so. Must be a drawer, I thought, after all, every lawyer is at least a second-rate doodler. The uninspiring nature of the legal pad would make anyone rush for the margins. When I told him I had been to a few of the countries of Central Asia he looked at me with disbelief. These were places that were only read about. Why would anyone go there when they could go anywhere else? He loved talking about Central Asia, but could not believe why anyone would go to the trouble of going.

"Why did you go there?"

I hesitated for a few moments and was somewhat unsure how to answer.

Again he said, "Why would you go across Central Asia?"

"I suppose...because it's there." Seeing that both he and I were unsatisfied with that answer, I tried to elaborate. "I just could not stand looking at the map anymore and not knowing what it was like there. I did not want a country or a culture to simply be a shape on a map or words in a book, I wanted it to be real. I wanted to see what those people looked like in person. That's how I ended up here in South America. It was a thought, I just felt I had to do it. I could not wonder anymore."

"Are you running?"

"Who isn't? I said somewhat startled, and defensively. And had to say more clearly, "who is not?"

"No, not me. I think you are running. I sit. I am sitting."

"Next to someone who is running?"

"Some people sit when they run."

"There is nothing to run from."

"I never said you were running from something. You are just a man who is running. Don't worry I'm sure its just a circle. A big circle."

He then drew a circle in the air in front of us with his finger.

"More like a triangle this time."

"I'm not saying it's bad, I want to run, too."

"From what?"

"Why do people always think running has to be running from something?"

"I don't know, it's just a common expression in America, I mean the U.S."

"No, running is just running. Like when you are a little kid and you find yourself running for no reason. To feel the wind. You are brave to travel to these places."

I had heard this before, and thought about it often, but there is nothing heroic about a traveler. Travelers are exotic to some people, and perhaps that's what I was to Italo. To the sedentary person or someone stuck in a place, the traveler is heroic and courageous, because they are doing something the other person has not or cannot. But the traveler is just a person that does not like to sit or is capable of leaving. A restless person. A wanderer.

While somewhat dazed from his sudden philosophizing, I realized Italo had closed the napkin map in his hand, thinking it would no longer suffice for our discussion. I reassured him that I liked and appreciated his map very much and enjoyed looking at maps in general. Besides, I still could not believe how accurate his map was. It was so specific, including mountains and rivers, with shading to indicate disputed regions and territories. I told him to open it up again so we could continue discussing the region.

He started up again with describing each place.

It was interesting to see how a line in a map meant the purposeful separation of different peoples. They were more than just lines, or just borders to him as well as to others. When a line connects to the middle of another and a border is created, there is more than just a physical border. Sometimes lines on a map were little more than a decision made by a few people, but the borders of the area he drew had cultural meaning.

There was something peculiar about crossing a border. Complexion and cultures completely different on each side of the line no matter how porous the border may be. Not only do the faces change but the customs, culture and politics can be completely different, too. It was a sudden change, similar to going in and out of Barrio Chino. He stuck the pen down on the borders of Kazakhstan and China. I had remembered this border well. Everything changed as soon as the train crossed into Kazakhstan and became wide open plains. "There was a dramatic difference between the dealing with the soldiers on the Chinese side than on the Kazakh side. The Kazakhs barely checked anything and were in and out in a matter of minutes. The Chinese had us sitting on that desolate border for hours. One man disappeared with our passports, only to reappear several times with questions and then taking off again. While we waited a number of young soldiers, searched through everything including computer files and USB keys. One young soldier even looked through each page of my notebooks and journals, asking personal questions. They loved looking at other people's stuff. The Kazakhs did not seem to care."

Italo then pointed to another place.

"You see this place, here? This is Fergana, in this valley it is dangerous and there is always a chance for rioting and violence because there are Kyrgyz inside of Uzbek territory. And right across the border is the city of Osh. Did you know there were riots in Osh and they tried to overthrow the government only a few years ago?"

I did know that, and I told him, "the only thing I had seen in the news about it was one or two articles and a video clip of a man running from a mob wielding flag poles, with the flags still on them, trying to swat him down. These countries are rarely heard about."

"About as much as Peru."

He was right, but again I felt the only well-mannered thing to do was to defend his country from him.

"But a lot of people come to Peru."

"Yes, but almost always to one place. Machu Picchu. They go see a beautiful pile of rocks next to the jungle, and then what?"

I tried not to agree with him, giving Peru its praises. But he was a man that had been stuck in this ghastly city the whole of his young life, most likely not in its nicer parts. There is more to Peru than Lima and Machu Picchu.

"Why did you come to Peru?"

"I guess, the same reason. Every country you've never been to is an interesting place. There is always a place in each country that people always visit. It's like in America, everyone wants to visit New York City." He appeared confused at a comparison between Machu Picchu and New York City, but I did not give up, "people see more of Peru than you think. I met travelers who had taken Ayahuasca up near Iquitos and surfed up and down the north coast, and some that had swum in the Amazon river near the border of Colombia." I realized he had not been to any of these places, as they almost sounded more distant than the Mongolia and Uzbekistan he spoke of with such interest.

"I went to Iquitos one time with some friends."

"I want to go up to Iquitos someday. There is supposedly a large butterfly farm nearby. Peru has more butterflies than any other country."

He smiled at the mention of butterflies, as most people do.

If he had not made me forget I was in Peru, he made me forget I was in Centro. We got caught up in the conversation of other places, not realizing where I was or how much time had passed, I suddenly realized that it was getting dark. Most every part of Centro outside the main square was a menacing place to be after dark, and some areas were not even worth going to during the day. The air is littered with the feeling that violence is never far. The buildings looked like places where unspeakable things happened, and people disappeared into. As relaxed as I was, I was for the most part alertly aware of the time of day, knowing to be away from the smaller and darker streets before sundown. The twilight felt like a ticking clock. I knew I could easily get lost and disoriented, no matter how well I knew the streets during the day. The constant overcast was confusing to the perception of time. It was four o'clock in the afternoon all day, thus near to the time I had to get back to my room. But I had been lost in conversation, talking about distant lands. Our discussion traveled around the world. We must have mentioned fifty different countries, and we both said something about each of them. We found common ground in our fascination with distant places that seemingly no one had heard of and less had been to. More importantly, it was interesting to know that someone else was interested in such places. We both saw people as being interesting in and of themselves. The way they looked, and how from time to time, perhaps more often than not, that it meant something or in some cases it had consequences.

I stood up knowing I needed to get back before the Centro completely put its night face on. Feeling like I was late for a plane, I worried of not making it to my flight early the next morning. I hurried the rest of the conversation and during a convenient pause, I said I had to be on my way. The expression on his face quickly became saddened that I would be leaving so suddenly, and he would have to return to talking to people he was familiar with. I was curt, but now I had a good reason. I did not want to navigate my way back to the main square in the lightless streets. It was almost an unspoken rule that Centro was a place that was off limits at night, no one needed to be told that to understand it. We quickly exchanged emails, and Italo stayed in the place he knew better than any other, more so than the places he had drawn so clearly for me on a napkin. He saw the urgency on my face and jokingly said, "Don't worry, you don't look as foreign as you think you do."

I laughed and said, "I have to run."

Lightning Source UK Ltd.
Milton Keynes UK
UKHW021901300120
357919UK00006B/160/J